Fairly Odd Mother

Fairly Odd Mother

Musings of a Slightly Off Southern Mom

Kelly Kazek

iUniverse, Inc.
New York   Bloomington

Fairly Odd Mother
Musings of a Slightly Off Southern Mom

The essays in this work previously appeared in *The News Courier*

iUniverse books may be ordered through booksellers or by contacting:

iUniverse
1663 Liberty Drive
Bloomington, IN 47403
www.iuniverse.com
1-800-Authors (1-800-288-4677)

ISBN: 978-1-4401-5706-6 (pbk)
ISBN: 978-1-4401-5707-3 (hc)
ISBN: 978-1-4401-5708-0 (ebk)

Printed in the United States of America

iUniverse Rev. 08/19/2009

To my most beautiful and patient daughter, Shannon –
you can pay me back some day in your own book.

And to Mom and Dad — wish you were here.

Contents

Note: The columns in this book were left in the Associated Press style in which they initially appeared in the newspaper. AP style varies slightly from those in English style manuals because it was created for brevity. As an English major myself (Auburn University, 1987), I know the urge may strike some of you to add a comma here or correct an abbreviation there so I readily give permission to mark up this book. Just don't write to tell me I don't know what I'm doing. I get enough of that already.

— Kelly Kazek

Acknowledgements

After several requests from readers to put a collection of my newspaper columns into a book, an idea was formed to create a community project to raise funds for two causes close to my heart: literature and newspapers.

Friends with Art on the Square in Athens, Alabama, through which a new branch was created to appreciate and support the art of the written word, supported the publication of this book and will receive a portion of proceeds for its projects. Many thanks to Art on the Square board members Alissa Rose-Clark, who also created the cover, and Diane Lehr, and to supporters J.R. Douthit, Bebe Gish Shaw and Michael Davis. Thanks also to cover model Emily Gordon.

Another portion of proceeds will go to help fund The News Courier's Newspapers in Education program to help bring newspapers into classrooms. Thanks to my publisher Ann Laurence for supporting my columns and to my colleagues mentioned on the following pages for letting me poke fun at them.

This book also would not have been possible without help from my friends and sometime editors Sabrina Holt, Charlotte Fulton and Traci Parker and Kim Rynders.

The columns themselves would not have been possible without the encouragement of my late parents, Charles and Gayle Caldwell; my grandmothers, Shannon Gray and the late Irma Caldwell; my brother, Kevin Caldwell; my aunt, Beverly Presley; and the inspiration of my daughter, Shannon Kazek.

And to my many readers who have written over the years to say a column made them laugh – that's the greatest gift. It's why I write.

Introduction

All mothers are slightly off — kids were born to make us that way.

The 2-day-olds in the hospital nursery — you know, the experienced ones —are whispering to the ones the nurses just brought in, "Psst. Hey, kid, here's the poop. When you get home, you start crying, see? They won't know why. They'll try the diaper, but you don't stop. They'll try to bottle, but you don't stop. They'll try rocking, but you don't stop. When they try the diaper again, stop, but only for a few minutes. Then start again but only 'til they try the bottle. Then, you should poop just for the heck of it. Try to make it a greenish color. It makes them all anxious. See how it works?"

While all moms may be a little nutty, Southern moms are a special breed.

In the South, we are proud of our nuts.

The rich folks, the ones with the houses that have verandas and columns — the real wooden kind, not those fake, hollow ones — call such relatives "eccentrics."

That's because they can afford to hide them behind expensive clothes, liquor and BMW convertibles.

Us regular folks, though still as proud, don't worry so much about hiding our nuts. We just let them walk around amongst ordinary folk and refer to them by such colorful phrases as "she's gone off her nut" or "the pilot light between her ears has gone out."

I don't know whether my family calls me nuts because that is something that would be said behind my back.

I do know that my teen daughter rolls her eyes and threatens that *if I write one more column about her ...*

The problem is, she is a lowly teenager and I, so far, have the power of the press behind me, so I told her I could understand her pain and humiliation and, as her loving mother, I say: tough.

A reader, though, came into the newspaper office a while back and was telling the clerk at the counter how much she enjoyed reading my columns. She loved to clip them and send them to her daughter in Michigan, she said.

Then the woman leaned forward and whispered conspiratorially: "But, tell me something," she said motioning the clerk closer. "Really. You can tell me. That Kelly Kazek ... she's not quite right, is she?"

The clerk, momentarily discombobulated and trying to remain professional, by which I mean keep from busting a gut, said, "Well, she keeps us laughing."

Our newsroom photographer Kim Rynders, upon hearing this story, said: "I woulda just told her: 'No, she ain't right!'"

Any-hoo. Hope this book keeps you laughing.

Section 1

So that's what grownups do all day

It ain't easy bein' cool when your name is Mom

(This section includes many columns about my daughter as a teenager, but also includes a few from when she was younger. They are not in chronological order).

Violence averted at O-Kazek Corral

The house was quiet.

I was in my bedroom; my daughter Shannon in hers.

Between us — the kitchen. Who would make the first move?

The tension mounted (cue the eerie, whistling theme to "The Good, The Bad and The Ugly.")

I unholstered my phone and dialed my teenage daughter's cell phone. Twenty-five feet away, from behind the closed bedroom door, she answered.

"Well?" I asked.

"Well?" she answered.

"Are you going to?"

"I said I would."

"That was two days ago. I want to know when."

"I said I would."

I waited. Still no sign of movement. In the kitchen, only the sound of crickets and passing tumbleweeds could be heard.

I decided to take action: I went to sleep.

In the morning, Shannon and I met at 20 paces in the kitchen.

"What's for breakfast?" she asked.

"No breakfast. Nothing to eat it from."

She shrugged, rolled up a chocolate-chip Eggo and went to catch her ride to school.

That night I was ready.

"Mom, I need a new outfit for Friday night."

I shrugged. "No money."

"No money?"

"No. Money."

She moved like a professional dish-slinger. I didn't even see her draw.

In fewer than two minutes, the dishwasher was empty.

I smiled and got my purse.

We went out for a nice mother-daughter shopping trip.

The standoff at the O-Kazek Corral had ended without bloodshed.

This time.

Welcome to the Booster Cult, er, Club

If you are the parent of a child between seventh and twelfth grades who has chosen— due to an excessive amount of school spirit, the desire to wear cute uniforms to attract the opposite sex, or an attraction to sniffing Sharpies — to join a school team of some sort, you may have received a letter like the one below.

If you haven't received yours in the mail yet, here's my advice: Move.

Just kidding. What I meant to say was, move *now*.

Typically, they go something like this:

Dear Parent (by which we mean person who has no clue what you've gotten yourself into),

Congratulations! Yippee-kay-yay High is thrilled your son/daughter made the cheer/band/basketball/dance/volleyball/soccer/football squad. We, the parents of the cheer/band/basketball/dance/volleyball/soccer/football boosters, want to welcome you to our little cult, er, club.

We want you to know, now that you can't ask your son/daughter to leave the squad without threat of a nuclear-level tantrum, that it will cost you approximately $25 to have your son/daughter on the team this year, before adding what we like to call "the little incidentals."

We know you'll agree that we can't possibly have a cheer/band/basketball/dance/volleyball/soccer/football squad without competing in the Hollywood Classic, and then the Nairobi Invitational. Sure, people think our mission is to perform/play to represent our school against other local schools, but they are stupid. The indoctrinated, er, experienced parent knows these are just *practices*. Our mission is to be able to say we kicked the world's butt.

So, when we say "little incidentals," we mean designer costumes/ uniforms — including four pairs of $200 shoes — airfare, accommodations, personalized sweat suits, team-logo duffles and spirit bags. These will total approximately $19,746.92. Oh, plus the $25 team-joining fee.

We Boosters realize some of you parents may be unable to afford this amount at one time, so, for a limited time only, we'll accept payments in four easy installments of $5,000 (we know this totals $20,000, but don't forget we must add those pesky handling fees!)

For those who still have trouble paying, never fear! We Boosters have planned 718 fundraisers (we prefer the term "spirit raisers!") between the first day of school and Christmas break so you will have the enjoyable team/ family building opportunity to raise the funds.

Spirit raisers include, but are not limited to, raffles, donut sales, car washes, beauty walks, cookie dough sales, the back-to-school festival, the Labor Day festival, the Columbus Day festival, the Veterans Day festival, the fall festival, the holiday festival and the Potato Growers Month festival.

These almost never take more than three weeks of preparation and usually only end up costing you about $290 in minor expenses such as cakes for the cake walk and checks you end up covering for relatives who forgot they ordered 48 rolls of wrapping paper complete with color coordinated bows.

Some of you may be thinking to yourselves: "I'd rather mortgage my house, stop buying groceries or harvest and sell my eggs than do fundraisers."

We Boosters say "pooh on you" but we make every effort to understand each individual family's, er, limitations. If you are not a dedicated stay-at-home mom who spins her own yarn to knit into stockings to sell at the holiday festival and spends time thinking of ways to cost parents more money, such as a team Christmas gift exchange or a secret pal program, if you work 40, even 50, hours per week, we will try to work with you.

For those parents, we allow exemptions from two spirit raisers, with an employers' or doctors' note.

Otherwise, all parents are required to be at these events three hours before start time to set up the cake walk or personalize with rhinestones Santa hats for the team to wear at the holiday festival.

We just know you will become a brainwashed, er, valued member of the Boosters and your son/daughter will be a cherished member of the cheer/ band/basketball/dance/volleyball/soccer/football team.

We know you won't disappoint any of us, including Booster masters, er, chairs, Lefty and Fingers McCoy.

Once again, welcome to the cheer/band/basketball/dance/volleyball/ soccer/football, where we're the best because we don't care about anything else!

See you at Booster orientation — and don't forget to bring your happy face!

Got dirt? Better call the UN

Did you know that we are suffering from a lack of dirt?

No, not here in the newsroom. We collect plenty of the stuff, and not just on the politicians.

But it seems the entire planet is lacking in dirt, according to a report from geologists published earlier this month in the Seattle Post-Intelligencer.

This statement may have made you, like me, scratch your head and say, "I thought the Earth was *made* of dirt."

In fact, some people use the words "dirt" and "earth" interchangeably (except, of course, Eartha Kitt).

I see lots of it in my daily activities, especially any time I wear white pants, when it just jumps right up on me, uninvited.

But apparently topsoil is being lost at the alarming rate of 1 percent per year and it is not being replenished.

The article specifically said "lost." Not stolen. Not a victim of foul play. Lost.

This begs the question: "Where could all this dirt be going?"

Outer space? Under a rug? Congress?

Before any more scientists waste brain cells, Red Bulls and taxpayer dollars trying to find the answer, I'll talk. I know where the dirt is — it's in my teenage daughter's closet.

Perhaps she was storing it in case mud wrestling made a comeback.

Perhaps she planned to start an earthworm farm.

I can't be sure. All I know is, she's been stockpiling dirt there since she was 2.

I hadn't been in the closet since 1999, but, searching for some old family photos the other day, I wondered if I dared risk it.

I moved slowly toward the closet, hearing the menacing theme from "Jaws" in my head as I approached. Facing the door, which suddenly seemed large and threatening, I muttered a prayer and turned the knob...

When I came to, I was lying in a pile of old shoes, toddler-size dresses, jigsaw puzzles, her rock collection, broken trophies, lint-covered Skittles, half-eaten Pop Tarts from 1995, green fuzzy stuff and 297 stuffed animals — all coated in dust and dirt.

Shannon, hearing my cries for help, ran to my side and cradled my head.

"Mom!" she yelled.

"I'll be OK," I muttered bravely.

"What are you doing going through my things?" she demanded, dropping my head, which hit a plastic Fisher-Price xylophone and bounced off. "Can't I get any privacy?!"

"Can you call 911?" I said weakly.

She continued: "And look at this mess! How will I ever get things organized again?"

Organized?

I didn't tell her but days later I sneaked outside the house and surreptitiously made a phone call to the United Nations, an organization which, according to the Post-Intelligencer, is on top of this whole dirt shortage thing.

What I did was difficult but necessary: I turned in my own daughter.

I told officials where they could find the Earth's missing dirt and told them if they wanted it, they could come get it.

All I asked is that they not hurt my daughter.

"She's just a child," I told them.

They said they'd come, right after they made another pick up at The National Enquirer.

Waiting for the dirt collection, I read the last few paragraphs of the article on dirt loss.

What I saw stunned me. Dirt, it said, "grows back."

Dirt *grows?!*

I pulled a blanket over my head and trembled.

And then, from the direction of the closet, I heard it.

Dun-uh. Dun-uh....

Take a page from the diary of a rocker mom

Ever wonder, if you're among the over-40 set, if you still have what it takes to attend a rock concert?

I got my answer last Saturday night when I escorted four 14-year-old girls to the Big Spring Jam in Huntsville, Alabama.

I knew my place was to stay far enough from them that none of their friends would realize they were being chaperoned while staying close enough to go running if one of them got hit in the head by a drunk, a stray guitar or a spray of rocker sweat.

Was it possible to survive four hours in this crowd without earplugs and a helmet?

I began to roam.

Hmmm. Interesting crowd.

Some cutesy preps in hair ribbons, some more worldly looking girls in does-your-mother-know-you-left-the-house-in-those shorts, guys who must have accidentally Super Glued their hands to the backs of those girls' shorts, and even a few people as wrinkled as Keith Richards.

Hey, that guy's hair looks interesting. Those spikes must be — what? — 18-inches high? Let's see, 18 inches times six spikes…I'd say that's at least a full jar of Dippity-do. Too high maintenance.

Hope he has a sunroof in his car.

Wonder where those pale-eyeliner-wearing people get those huge-mongous black pants with all those zippers and chains. The ones with legs wide enough to swallow small dogs or manhole covers. I've never seen any of those in J.C. Penney. Maybe there's a huge-mongous-black-manhole-cover-pants warehouse somewhere.

Would ya look at that? I've never seen a cowboy hat made from a Coors box before. Shouldn't that guy be at the country music stage? Or maybe the Talladega 500? This band doesn't even play "Sweet Home Alabama."

He's headed over to the porta potty corral — with 16 of them in a row like that, you'd think the lines would be shorter.

Will I need to go in the next hour or so? I better decide now because that's how long the wait looks.

Guess I'd better not give too much thought to those porta potties.

Wish I had one of those astronaut diapers.

Did that lead singer just say the F-word? Where is his mother? If I had a bar of soap…

Will my ears be ringing like this tomorrow? Or maybe that's how the music's supposed to sound.

What's that shirt say? "Boobies make me smile." Tsssk. Isn't that just like a guy? Wait a minute.

That's no guy.

Maybe I'll head up this grassy knoll and look down on the crowd. That way I can keep an eye on the girls. Ahh. It's nice up here. Not too much smoke. If I lie back I can almost see the stars through the haze. Wait, better sit up. I don't want to fall asleep and wake up on the back of one of those little tractor doo-hickeys they're using to cart away passed out people.

That could be hard to explain.

Oh, no. More porta-potties.

I'll hum to myself so I won't have to think about it.

"Like a bridge over troubled water…"

Bad choice.

"Oh black water, keep on rollin'…"

Even worse.

What's that sound? Silence. Almost didn't recognize it.

Finally, we can leave and find a real bathroom.

"High five, man!" someone shouts. Seems I'm the "man" judging by the sweaty, shirtless, tattooed guy holding his palm toward me.

I slap it, then rub my hand on my jacket. Maybe the guy's taking pity on the old person at the rock concert but I like to think he doesn't notice I don't belong.

"Wow! That was awesome!" the girls say as we begin the half-mile trek to the car, with me walking really fast toward relief. "Did you see those people crowd surfing? That was the best night ever."

Yeah, for me, too. Just don't say "surf."

Next time, I won't forget the astronaut diaper.

Escape to Never Never Smell Stinky Feet Again Land

Someone has been in my house.

He is watching my daughter and me.

He stalks our every move, waiting until late at night when we've changed for bed. Then he makes his move — and takes our socks.

On a recent trip to Wal-Mart, I bought two 10 packs of white socks, one for my daughter Shannon and one for me. I got the cheapest packs possible because, in roughly two weeks' time, I will need to buy more.

The stalker can't keep his hands off our footwear.

It was only about two weeks ago that I bought Shannon a six-pack and, by the eighth day, I noticed she had set out a pair of brown socks to wear. I knew she didn't own brown socks, so I looked closer. Yep, they were once white.

I picked up one. It was stiff.

"Why are you wearing these nasty socks?" I asked her.

She shrugged.

"Go get one of your new pair and I'll attempt to wash these. I might be able to get them to a nice shade of beige," I said.

"I'll just wear these again," Shannon said, taking the brittle sock and forcing it onto her foot.

There could be only one reason she would take the fashion risk of wearing brown socks with her black sweater.

"Have you lost all your new socks again? Already?"

"I didn't *lose* them," she said defensively. "I just can't find any of them."

"Did you look under your bed? In the closet? What about in that pile of dirty clothes hidden behind the door?"

"I looked everywhere, Mom," she said. She shrugged again. "They're just gone."

I checked my own sock drawer only to discover I was also down to one pair.

I know this problem is not unique to our home; moms have complained about the mysterious sock-eating monster for centuries. In fact, it is such a widely known problem that companies sell products to clip socks together so one will not "disappear" in the washer.

Still, I am mystified.

On Saturday, when Shannon was out of the house, I searched her room myself.

I found my good silver necklace and 25 ponytail holders, even some cat-fur-coated Skittles, but no fresh white socks.

In the laundry room, I looked in the hamper, behind the washer, in the lint trap.

In the kitchen, I looked in the pantry, in the sugar canister, in the 'fridge (hey, at our house, it could happen; I found shampoo in there once).

In the den, I looked between sofa cushions and under the computer desk.

I even looked in the litter box in the garage.

Nada.

I pondered. Even if all the socks in our home had managed to fall behind cushions or under beds, surely they would have to surface. I figured after 12 years in our home I should have come across a large pile of once-worn socks at some point.

I imagine they would now number in the thousands.

Is our house in the center of a Bermuda Triangle-like zone, where socks go in but they don't come out?

Or do washers actually have trap doors that whisk socks (never T-shirts or bras) to Never, Never Smell Stinky Feet Again Land?

A place where socks frolic free of children's sweaty feet and where no one throws them in dark corners where bugs lurk? Or where they are not torn into rags and never again become a dog's play toy, tugged at by pointed teeth and coated in dog breath?

It's a happy thought.

For the socks.

But not for my tormented child, limping around in brittle, brown-ish socks.

I'm planning to stay up late tonight, aiming the video camera at my sock drawer. I still have eight pairs from my new pack and I plan to fight for them.

But if I find our socks are escaping to some island where the sun shines all day and feet never smell, you might have to come looking for me. I'll be the one stuck in the washing machine, looking for paradise.

So that's what grownups
do all day

I got up Friday morning hoping my daughter Shannon still would be fast asleep.

I derive most of my day's pleasure from repeatedly yelling into her room: "Get up or we're going to be late for school!"

On a good day, she is sleeping so soundly that I get to go into her room and nudge her awake.

"Mo-o-om!" she whines in annoyance. It's my favorite sound.

Then, I proceed to ask Shannon what she's going to wear and if it needs ironing.

Reminding her to eat her breakfast is fun, but not as much fun as yelling, "Five minutes! Brush your teeth and I mean good!" I dread the day when she remembers to do these things for herself because I won't get to yell quite so much in the mornings.

We rush to the car, making both of us stressed, which is good because that's the best way to start another day of sixth grade.

In the car line at school, I give Shannon a kiss and yell, "I love you, Doodlebug!" as loudly as I can so the other kids will hear me and make fun of her.

Once at work, the pressure is off. My co-workers and I get some cones from Kreme Delite and play a game of Twister.

After lunch, we run with scissors and make prank calls to the mayor's office asking if his FAX machine is running. Yes? "Well, you better go catch it," I say, tickled at my joke.

Then, I spend a couple of hours shopping using my checkbook. As long as there are plenty of checks in there, I can buy whatever I want.

After work, I come home tired. Who wouldn't after a day like that?

While I sit on the sofa, I make Shannon do the dishes and pick up the clothes on her bedroom floor.

I never do any of the work. What does she think I had a kid for?

"Oh, and Doodlebug?" I call to her. "Could you hand me the remote to the TV?"

While watching Shannon work is highly entertaining, it can't compete with my favorite time of day: bath time. She tells me she just bathed two days ago before soccer practice and dance class so I get to nag until she's squeaky clean and has washed her hair.

Finally, it's time for bed. I start telling Shannon to go to bed at 8:30, but I secretly hope she'll stay up late so I can have fun yelling again in the morning.

This is how I think my child imagines my day. She thinks everything I do is calculated to make her life more difficult. If I can wait her out, though, I suspect it will be only about 10 years or so before she rethinks things. Once she's out of college and on her own, she may give me a call.

"Mom? Can I move back home? I keep oversleeping and I got fired from my job, where, by the way, they made me actually work. Plus, I'm tired of eating frozen macaroni and cheese every night. And those checks? Did you know they're only good if there's money in your bank account?"

And I'll tell her, "Sure. Come on home. We'll play Twister and make some prank calls."

Daughter has to keep mom on course

My daughter was born with GPS. Don't send get well cards — it's not a gastrointestinal problem.

I mean she has an incredible sense of direction, her own global positioning system.

I can't imagine where she gets it — her mother is directionally dyslexic. (I'll have to be satisfied she got her good looks and incredible sense of style from me).

If I am in the passenger's seat and the driver asks me which way to turn, I will repeat "right, right, right" all the while motioning left.

Shannon suggested writing an "L" and an "R" on the toes of my shoes. Smart-aleck kid.

When Shannon was 7 or 8, she held out her hand and stared silently at me until I agreed to turn over all maps. On road trips, I now defer to her ability to know where, exactly, she is on the planet at any given moment.

Before I was willing to admit my problem, we lost countless hours on road trips driving 40 miles to the next exit so we could turn around (why they can't put turnarounds every 100 feet, I don't understand. Those highway people punish every little miscalculation by making us drive until there is a Stuckey's).

"Mom," Shannon would sigh. "You *always* get lost."

"Lost? What lost? Can't you see from that sign right there we are approaching exit 259 on Interstate 75 north?" Who knew you needed to head south to get to Florida?

Then I'd buy her a pecan log from Stuckey's to keep her from blabbing to my dad that I made a teensy-weensy miscalculation — again.

If Shannon only knew the real meaning of the word: lost is wandering in the woods with only one piece of chocolate in your pocket and no idea which way the campground snack machine is, lost is passing a ski lift on your way to the beach, lost is walking through the mall with no money in your checking account.

These are situations that leave you feeling utterly hopeless.

The other night, Shannon and I got in the car so I could take her to a dance team party at the home of a teammate I'd never met. At the entrance of our subdivision, I realized I didn't have a clue where we were going.

"I forgot the directions," I said, preparing to turn around.

"That's OK, Mom," Shannon said. "I read the e-mail. You turn right into Wall Farms subdivision, take a left at the first stop sign, right at the second brick house, right at the big oak and it's the third house on the right, the one with the red garage door."

"You remember all that from reading the e-mail? How?"

"Easy," she says. "I just picture the route in my head —visualizing things helps you avoid mistakes. You should try it. Like before leaving the house next time, try visualizing how those pants will look with that top."

Smart-aleck kid.

A single mom's ~~nightmare~~ dream before Christmas

'Twas the week before Christmas, and all through the halls,
Nothing was ready for old Santa Claus;
Decorations lay scattered across the sofa and chairs
The cat sat on one, then flew through the air;

My kid wouldn't help; she had plans, you see;
For outings and parties, but what about me?
When I did get invited, I have to confess,
I could not find a listing for the man named "Plus Guest"

So I maneuvered alone through the holiday mire
Unclogging the toilet with hooks and some wire;
Washing the clothes that were piled on the floor
In a stack so high it was blocking the door;

I dusted the shelves; I cleared away clutter
But one glance at the baseboards made me shudder;
Cat fur was nestled down in the cracks,
A table was marked with a telltale scratch;

I knew the trio who held the blame,
So I whistled and shouted and called them by name;
"Bad Luvey, bad Scout and you too, Mad Max,
Don't think I don't recognize your dirty paw tracks."
They looked one-by-one, then slowly blinked,
Then laid down to get another 500 winks;

When finally the room was suitably clean,
I got ready to completely destroy it again;
I pulled out the lights from an old attic box
Mangled and tangled into masses of knots;

For six hours I worked to solve the riddle,
And found the problem was bubblegum stuck in the middle;
Then I borrowed a truck, and returned with a tree,
Hollered: "It's time to decorate" enthusiastically;
"Can't. Got a game," the answer came back,
So I did it myself, with some help from Mad Max.

I flopped on the sofa, too tired to move,
And wondered why moms have so much to prove;
"I can't do it all," I yelled, sounding bitter;
"I wish, for one day, I had just *me* to consider."
I was drifting to sleep, though my muscles were aching,
When I heard a soft tinkling like the sound of glass breaking;

I jumped up; prepared with a colorful shout
My squirt gun loaded and ready for Scout;
Then what to my tired swollen eyes did appear,
But a man all in black who filled me with fear;
"Wait!" the man said, as I aimed to shoot,
He wiped off the soot and I saw a red suit;

"Is that you, Santa?" I asked, amazed
"But it's not Christmas for another six days."
Shaking his head, he pulled out a list,
"I came to grant your holiday wish,"
"The one where you asked to be by yourself
When you didn't wash dishes or dust off the shelf,
Which day do you want? I'll make the cats disappear
I'll put Shannon to work washing reindeer."

For a moment or two, we considered each other,
But I couldn't give up one day as a mother;
Though I thought I would like having no one to boss
I knew without family, I would be lost;

"I couldn't accept; I'd feel like a heel,
But Santa," I said. "Could we make a deal?
Could I have just one hour with no chores to do,
No errands to run, no bills past due,
Sixty small minutes with no cats meowing,
No one to impress, no boss who needs wow-ing,
Just one single hour with no one to keep,
An hour, perhaps, when I could just sleep?"

Santa ho-hoed; I saw a deep dimple;
"That's all?" he asked. "Why, sure, that's simple."
He lay his finger aside of his nose,
Quick as a wink, I was deep in a doze;

I dreamed of a time when I wasn't in charge,
When I could go on wild trips in a snazzy sports car;
It would happen sometime, some way or another,
When I could finally say I was a grandmother!

Then from far, far away, Santa called from his sleigh,
"You've earned a long nap, you work hard each day,
And to all single moms whose days are quite harried,
May your nights be silent and your Christmas be merry!"

Mom dares to dream about sharing teen's clothes

Some think of joy as the sound of a baby's laughter or the look of wonder on a child's face on Christmas morning.

On my planet, joy is removing the belt from my pants after a hard day's work and realizing I accidentally put on the belt of my 14-year-old daughter that morning— and it fit!

Not only that, but I wore it all day and had no trouble breathing or walking down stairs. I didn't even have to unbuckle it after wolfing down a lunch of Lean Cuisine, Diet Coke and six peanut-butter, chocolate-chip cookies.

I trembled at the realization that I existed, even for one day, in the belt of a size 1.

Since I began losing weight a year ago, I have joked with my daughter Shannon that we soon would be wearing each other's clothes. It's every mother's dream — not only to be the same size as her daughter, but to have her clothes deemed stylish enough to meet a teen's standards.

But with me still a size 10, it seemed an unattainable dream, an unreachable star, a preposterous, unachievable utopia. More unrealizable, I thought, than my dream of living on an island populated only by Orlando Bloom and trees that drip chocolate.

Now it's closer than I thought possible. Sharing a belt was only the beginning.

Soon the joyous day dawned when Shannon hollered: "Mom! I don't have anything to wear under this shirt and it's too low cut."

I realized the size-medium black tank I wear under low-cut tops would fit her without falling off. Heart racing, I grabbed the shirt and handed it to her. Trying to sound casual, I said, "Here. Try this."

I waited, breath held, until she emerged from her room wearing the tank beneath her top.

"Thanks, Mom," she said.

Tears sprang to my eyes. Without realizing it, my baby had just made her mother's millennium. She had borrowed my clothes.

Never mind the top is so tight on me it rides up above the muffin-top created by my gut when the waist of my pants is too snug. Never mind she was wearing it under another top so the fit didn't have to be the best.

She was still dressed in my clothes for the very first time.

It was a moment. No one can take it from me.

Still, it may be a while before Shannon and I achieve maximum clothes-swappage.

A few months back, when I reached a size reasonable enough, I followed Shannon into the junior's department to look at some hip-looking blouses.

"Mo-o-o-om," Shannon said, rolling her eyes. "You can't shop here." (She also advised me later that *absolutely no one* uses the word "hip" anymore, but that's a subject for another day).

"Why not?" I asked. "It's not like I'm planning to wear micro-minis or belly shirts. I just thought some of these tops were cute. I promise to stay age-appropriate."

"But someone I know might see you here," she said, in a tone suggesting I had somehow morphed into Forrest Gump. "Besides, what if I like the same top? We *can't have the same top.*" There was now a hint of desperation in her voice.

"I promise to give you first choice," I said. "If you like it, I promise I won't buy it."

She was partially mollified.

I added: "And I won't shop in the junior department until you've gone to another store."

Seeming to accept this shift in our relationship — her new lot in life — she moved among the clothing racks while I moseyed across the aisle to look at the jewelry.

I sighed.

Just across the aisle lay my hopes for the future. But I'm patient. I can wait.

If I lay off those post-lunch cookies, I might one day get to wrestle Shannon for the last pair of size-nothing, hip-hugging jeans on the sale rack.

A mom can only dream.

Teaching teen to drive may require duct tape, Depends

Y'all, if you see me out somewhere and I inexplicably begin to stomp my right foot, please refrain from calling for emergency medical personnel or a tranquilizer gun.

It's just a nervous habit I've picked up since my daughter Shannon turned 15 and the State of Alabama, in its infinite wisdom as demonstrated by our high ranking in education, decided she was old enough to operate two tons of steel and leather-look plastic powered by a fickle computer and a massive engine.

Who, in the name of all that is good and holy and sane, decided 15 was old enough?

It took Shannon three years to learn to color inside the lines. Now the state thinks one year is enough for her to learn to drive inside the lines — and the stakes are a little higher. When she strayed from the lines in coloring, she might miss out on a smiley-face sticker, but at least she wouldn't end up in a hospital.

I told myself I was prepared for this.

I would not be one of those mothers who white knuckled the ceiling strap my best friend used to call the "Oh hell" handle.

I would not scream, "Watch out!" and grab the steering wheel when crossing five lanes of traffic.

And I certainly would never, under any circumstances, stomp the passenger-side floorboard in hopes it would pop out and I could use foot brakes á la Fred Flintsone in an effort to stop the car and the madness.

But during the first month of riding shotgun, my standards have changed.

Now the only rule is: Don't look.

Let me make one thing clear (in case she's reading this): Shannon is actually a very good driver. When she was 14, I took her to the church parking lot at night and to undeveloped subdivisions to let her drive where none of the targets were living.

She mastered basic vehicle operations and, to her credit, she never so much as hit a single construction Dumpster or dinged a "Reserved for Pastor" sign.

Thanks to that training, she can drive the heck out of empty lots and vacant streets.

But then came the first time she would drive on an actual road with actual lanes meeting actual cars driven by actual people.

It was dark. First mistake.

We were on a heavily traveled road with no shoulder. Second mistake.

I didn't realize one important skill Shannon could not learn in a church parking lot was how to judge the distance between our car and Certain Death.

I tried to stay calm as the right-side tires rode the white line and I stared at the dark shapes of trees whizzing past the passenger window and the deep ditch that was inches away.

We were a few miles from home when Shannon said: "Um, Mom, it makes me nervous when you keep grabbing that handle."

Well. We wouldn't want Sweet'ums to be nervous, would we?

We survived and the very next day we made our first foray onto a four-lane U.S. highway.

I realized another thing Shannon did not learn in the church parking lot: The meaning of all those red lights on the backs of cars.

"Slow down!" I hollered.

"I *was* slowing down," she replied, a little too calmly to soothe my last, frayed nerve, to which I was now clinging tighter than the "oh, hell" handle. She eyed my foot as it stomped the floor, then rolled her eyes dramatically, which was way too much extracurricular activity for eyes that were supposed to be glued to the road.

Later, when we were safely parked at a 45-degree angle in the Target parking lot and I had kissed the pavement, I told Shannon she was doing a good job.

"Then why do you keep stomping and grabbing and yelling?"

I guess actions speak louder than words.

I'll have to try a new approach.

I'm thinking of wearing Depends and some duct tape over my mouth.

If that doesn't work, maybe a blindfold — oh, and a shot from that tranquilizer gun.

Mamas, don't let your babies grow up to be brats

This new breed of super mamas has me all fired up.

You know the ones I mean. Those perfectly coifed, mani/pedi-ed mothers who make sure nothing is ever amiss in the lives of their offspring, raising kids who have to take deep breaths into their lunch bags if the crusts were not removed from their PB&Js and who want Mama to call the principal if someone put them out at kickball during recess.

Look, I understand spoiling your kid. Mine is walking around with a brand-new, $200 cell phone you can make dinner reservations and check stock quotes from while I am using a 5-year-old phone whose display stopped working two months ago so I am never sure if I'm dialing Nanna or 1-900-HOT-DUDES.

I'm not talking about a little harmless spoiling. I'm talking about Mamas who are so worried their Precious Babies might get their feelings hurt they instill in them a sense of entitlement, such as the belief they are entitled to have their hair regularly highlighted at the salon starting at age 10 — something I can't even afford more than once a year.

This phenomenon starts in preschool when mamas try to make their children more popular by outdoing the other mamas.

If you have kids, you have likely witnessed one of these mama smackdowns.

If little Sally brings pink princess cupcakes to school for a class party, then Marcie's mom has to make a chocolate cake with gummy worms baked inside for Halloween. My friend from Birmingham said some of those Big City Mamas have started decorating their babies' elementary school lockers with marabou and sequins. All those scrapbookin' mamas must have had heart palpitations when they saw rows of blank locker doors.

Well, we wouldn't want the kids to be ill-prepared for book-learnin' by being forced to use bland lockers.

And as we've witnessed on the MTV show "My Sweet Sixteen," more and more girls feel the need to arrive at birthday parties on the backs of elephants or brand new pink BMW convertibles.

I say if you want to enter a party on an elephant, you should have to earn it. But that's just me.

It's all well and good to want your child to have the finer things in life. Shannon eats better, dresses better and gets invited to better parties than me. Not that I'm bitter.

But some of these Mamas need to be reminded of their Southern roots before the situation gets out of hand.

Sure, we spent most of our childhoods learning to be pretty, perfect and pleasant but no one should confuse this with weakness. Where do you think the phrase "steel magnolias" comes from?

Behind every prim Southern young'un was a girl who could outspit her fourth-grade boyfriend and outmaneuver an overly aggressive date without wrinkling her dress.

Southern mamas used to know when someone was getting too big for her britches.

Southern mamas used to know you can be pretty and act ugly at the same time and, if you get caught acting ugly, you aren't too big to take a switch to.

So when we start writing their English papers and insisting coaches put them in the game just so they'll never have to suffer disappointment, we have gone too far. As our mamas used to say, we've rurn't 'em.

All the marabou and sequins in the scrapbook kit can't disguise a rurn't kid.

Mom gets dumber as teen ages

Only yesterday, I was pretty smart.

Yep, I had managed to get a college degree and a fairly respectable job, plus I could figure out the correct answers on "Wheel of Fortune" before Vanna turned over the last letter.

I even knew not to use the blow dryer while in the bathtub or date middle-aged men who still live with their mothers.

I felt I had a lot of wisdom to impart to my daughter, like: "Never let a man see you put on control top pantyhose" (or, for that matter, take them off. Someone could get hurt).

And for many years, I was smart enough to know the correct answers to Shannon's every question, at least as far as she knew.

But on one recent day, not long before Shannon's 15th birthday, I awoke stupid. I suddenly was an idiot, a dunce, superdork, someone about as sharp as a buttermilk biscuit.

Not only am I too dense to know good music when it vibrates my car and the houses on both sides of the road, I am too slow to understand why Shannon can't possibly clean her room and still have time to apply makeup and fix her hair before Britney's party, and too dense to know why her 11:30 p.m. curfew makes her appear childish among her friends.

It seems I get dumber the older Shannon gets and, this will astonish you, my IQ drops exponentially when I am in the *presence of more than one teen.*

Whenever Shannon has a friend around there is so much eye rolling that I expect at any moment to see one of 'em pop out and roll across the floor.

Suddenly, every comment I make is so, like, totally juvenile.

Really, I'm beginning to think I don't deserve to drive her around and buy her stuff.

Just the other day, I turned down the volume on the car radio — a song I "don't get" because the lyrics rhyme "low" with "more" and talk a lot about "lady lumps" — to tell Shannon and her friend Alli something I'd seen on TV that morning, an item about Fergie (see, I'm not too stupid to recognize a Black-Eyed Pea when I see one).

Shannon's response to my timely and newsworthy commentary?

A bored: "Well, that was five minutes I'll never get back."

She was joking.

I think.

If only I were smart enough to recognize sarcasm.

A few seconds later, Shannon asked: "Can you turn the CD back on, Mom?"

"Nah," I said. "That song wasted five minutes I'll never get back. That's a mistake I won't let happen again, thanks to your insight."

Shannon was discombobulated (I'd like to see the teenager who can use *that* word correctly in a sentence).

With the music held hostage — a result of the indisputable international rule that the driver controls the radio dials — I was once again brilliant in my daughter's eyes.

Suddenly, she was overflowing with praise.

Sure, Shannon soon will have a driver's permit but for another year at least, I control the keys to the car.

I'm sure when she hits the road in a year's time, my insights about looking both ways, checking the rearview mirror and using a turn signal will seem even more stupid.

But I'm patient.

When she heads off to college and has to balance a checkbook, do laundry and get to class on time, Mom's advice might start looking pretty smart.

Then one day, a *lo-o-o-ong* time after college, she'll have a daughter of her own.

And on that day, I'll once again be the smartest person in her universe.

Darn kids keep changing the rules on parents

No one told me when I became a parent that the rules would keep changing.

Had I known, I might have given the situation more careful consideration.

When Shannon was in ninth grade, I pulled to the curb to drop Shannon at a friend's house. I waved hello to her friend Faith, who was standing outside with two boys from their school.

"Mo-o-om," said Shannon. "Don't *wave*."

I was befuddled.

I knew not to pick her up while wearing a green, moisturizing facial mask and curlers in my hair.

I knew not to create a MySpace account and invite her group to join my Friends list.

I knew not to holler, "Pick you up at 8, Doodlebug."

I even knew not to spit on my fingers and smooth her bangs in public.

I didn't know not to wave.

When she was in eighth grade, waving was permissible.

Without a rulebook, how are we parents supposed to keep up?

I tried reminding Shannon that I manage to follow more rules than some of her friends' parents, like the mom who wipes her daughter's cheeks and says, "That blush makes you look like a Hollywood streetwalker."

On behalf of moms everywhere, I decided to start my own list, one we can use to remind our kids they were embarrassing us long before they felt the need to ride to school in the trunk so they can say, "My mom? No, that's just some woman who tried to kidnap me on the way to school."

After interviewing a few other moms on the subject, I compiled a partial list:

1. At age 1, smiled adorably from the store shopping cart before spewing a substance that looked like curdled potato soup on Mommy's two-day-old black suede jacket. Customers ran; stout woman slipped on spewage and an ambulance was called. The woman survived; the jacket did not.

2. At age 2, returned from a trip to the restaurant bathroom with Mommy and loudly announced to the group of friends at the table: "I went poo-poo in the potty." People at next table applaud, but leave without eating.

3. Age 3, did a strip tease in preschool bawdy enough to rival the Paris Hilton tape. Parents of three little boys threatened sexual harassment lawsuits.

4. Age 5, after overhearing Mommy whisper to a friend while in line at the bank, said loudly, "Mommy, I don't think that lady's hairdo makes her look like Cyndi Lauper on crack."

5. Age 6, when asked by first grade teacher to draw a picture of your family engaged in favorite activities, drew Mommy drinking a glass of wine and watching soap operas and Daddy scratching his stomach and burping. Hung on the wall in the first grade hallway for a month.

Feel free to clip the list to use during the next argument with your teen. You probably still won't win, but at least you'll no longer be unarmed.

Seventies music was awesomely, terribly wonderful

When you tell your teenager hard truths, you have to expect some resistance. This is why, on a recent road trip, my daughter looked at me incredulously, by which I mean the same way she looks at me whenever I dare speak to her in public.

But this time, she was eloquent in her disbelief: "Nuh-uh," she said, her stare challenging me.

I knew then she would need proof that there was, indeed, a song lamenting the loss of a perfectly good cake that someone had, either unwittingly or as part of some maniacal terrorist plot, left out in the rain.

This time, my word would not be enough.

I have spent many years trying to school Shannon in the terrible awesomeness that was the 1970s, when women were strong, they were invincible despite — or perhaps because of — the invention of Daisy Duke cutoffs, and songs were brilliant in their badness, glorious garbage that managed to get stuck in your head until you would happily use an ice pick to remove it.

Anyone who has ever sung about going to the desert on a horse with no name, or about Muskrat Sam ticklin' the fancy and rubbin' the toes of Muskrat Susie without even questioning what they were saying knows how invasive this music could be. It was like being brainwashed into a pop-music cult.

The public's response to a great many songs of the '70s was: "Were they droppin' acid when they wrote that?"

And then: "Cool."

My most recent example for Shannon was the song "MacArthur Park," as covered by a gold-laméd Donna Summer in 1977:

"Someone left the cake out in the rain;
And I don't think that I can take it;
'Cause it took so long to bake it;
And I'll never have that recipe again….oh, no!"

I am guessing it was a rum cake, or at the very least had chocolate amaretto icing. What other cake would be so painful in its loss?

Even then, it is difficult to believe that:

A. Someone wrote these lyrics

B. Someone put them to music

And C. Someone offered to sing them in actual public — and did not even have the decency to look embarrassed.

But even more distressing is the fact that I *know all the words.*

I played the 45 rpm (for you youngsters, that's a small black record with a hole in the middle that was played on a machine given the technical name "record player" that did not have the capability of vibrating an entire city block with its bass) until one day it disappeared from my room, leaving me to surmise my mother finally broke down, took it in the backyard and pumped it full of heavy metal from my brother's BB gun.

Rather than admit to Shannon I spent the better part of my 12th year singing lyrics that could be construed as ravings of a rabies-infected Julia Child, I tried to give them meaning.

Perhaps the writer had been traumatized as a child by a fiendish birthday clown who soaked his cake with a squirting lapel flower.

Perhaps the lyrics were a metaphor for a lost love — one with a serious whipped cream fetish.

Finally, I gave up.

"Fine. It's a really stupid song, OK?" I admitted to Shannon. "But let's be clear here: It's really, really fun to sing in the car with the windows down. Just be sure you *never* let anyone hear you."

'YMCA' is inherently dangerous song

After introducing my daughter to the glories of cake left in the rain with the 1970s version of "MacArthur Park," we had a discussion in the newsroom about favorite songs from our youth.

I learned there are times you should keep your past to yourself, lest you be labeled odd.

For instance, should you really ever tell people — even close friends or spouses — that you can still remember all the words to Michael Jackson's "Ben?"

I recently found a recording of the song on YouTube (did you know you can find anything there, even rarely heard recordings like the theme song from the old children's show "The Banana Splits" and Paris Hilton songs?)

I played "Ben" for Shannon, who's 15:

"Ben, the two of us need look no more;
we both found what we were looking for…"

I said to her: "You'll never guess who he's singing about."

From her more contemporary standpoint, Shannon guessed: "Some little kid?"

Hmmm.

But no, this was Michael Jackson of the 1970s — hip, cool and still black. He was singing, I told Shannon, about a…rat. "Ben" was the theme song for a horror film.

She shrugged.

I guess when you listen to songs about "lovely lady lumps," an ode to a friendship with a rat doesn't seem so odd.

My coworkers who are a tad younger have been caught rolling their eyes at '70s music, as if those Black-Eyed Butter Bean people are so-o-o-o much better. So when I had the opportunity to take one of our young reporters I'll call Jennifer Hill — mainly because thatís her name — on a road trip to an Alabama Press Association convention, I gathered all my CDs from the '70s. On the trip with me were 20-something Jennifer, Shannon and her friend Mackenzie.

They wanted to listen to hip-hop music.

I was more than willing to listen to their requests, then reminded them that I had the keys and, well, tough.

What we learned from this experience was that the '70s churned out loads of crowd-pleasing music and people look at you funny when you pull up to a red light rockin' Rick Springfield's "Jessie's Girl."

As it turned out, everyone in the car could sing along to my Disco Gold CD. (What? I said it. "Disco Gold." I refuse to be ashamed.)

We rolled down the windows and sang along to "I Will Survive," "Car Wash" and the ultimate disco classic, "YMCA." BTW, you really should never play "YMCA" in a moving vehicle because, well, there is an inherent element of danger.

Don't ask me how I know this.

Suffice it to say:

1. It is impossible to hear the song without making the accompanying hand motions;
2. The accompanying hand motions require removing your hands from the steering wheel;
3. Police aren't always understanding when you explain you veered into the next lane because you were steering with your knees.

My young companions thought I monopolized the CD player but really, let's be honest, could we have rolled down the window and sung "Baby Got Back" or "Ms. New Booty?"

I think not — at least not without the threat of arrest.

So a good time was had by all, plus we had the added excitement of devising a new invention.

We could patent a small, magnetized scrolling computer screen, much like those seen at banks, to place on the sides of cars that would announce what songs drivers were listening to.

It could be very beneficial to see "YMCA" flash on the screen and know that driver is steering with her knees.

Meanwhile, until I get the patent, you might want to avoid anyone driving a black Honda.

What? I can't help myself.

You might have a teenager if...

It snowed last week.

OK, it wasn't snow so much as a 10-minute flurry of something wet and white-looking. But when 10 white flakes fall from the sky in Alabama, we get all excited.

Sometimes, I like to throw some bleached oatmeal in the air just to see if I can cause a rush to supermarkets for milk, fire logs and National Enquirers.

Everybody's gotta have a hobby.

This time, when it was real snow, I called my 15-year-old daughter Shannon, who was home because of a school holiday. She has always loved snow, even though she only saw it accumulate once when she was 3. Whenever we'd have flurries, she'd run outside to watch.

"It's snowing!" I told her.

"Mmmrrmph," she said.

"Are you sleeping?"

"Mmmrrrmmrmph," she replied.

"You can't even wake up to go see the snow?"

No response, just a light snoring and what I thought might be the sound of drool hitting the phone.

I hung up, feeling a bit older and more than a little jaded.

It was like having to wake Shannon on Christmas morning to open gifts — she had reached an age where she'd rather sleep than play in the snow!

When did that happen?

Probably at the same time she began sleeping until noon on Saturdays, eating her weight in pasta and sending long, detailed text messages with one finger.

Just so no other parent is surprised, I've compiled warning signs that your child officially has become a teen.

You might be a teenager if...

- You need an archaeologist to find the floor of your room or a clean pair of underwear;
- You clean your room by throwing everything into the wash, whether or not it's dirty;
- You only wake up if food or a phone call from a boy is involved;
- You would rather text than do anything other than eat;
- Sometimes will text while eating;
- Your bathtub has a black ring that no amount of bleach or sandpaper will remove;
- You are not amused that your mom knows words to the latest hip-hop song;
- You believe curfews are stupid and everyone should just lighten up and start school later so you can sleep in — say 1 p.m. or so;
- You believe your mom requires supervision anytime she goes near the computer, cell phone or DVD player;
- You think you are responsible enough to drive a car but not to empty the kitty litter;
- You have enough energy to stay up until 3 a.m. at sleepovers and shop for four hours straight but you have to text your mom from the bedroom to ask her to bring you something to drink.

These attributes can be expected to last from one year or until the teen is well into her 20s. But don't worry. At 18, she becomes the college professor's problem.

It's not just teen drivers who need warning labels

Legislators are bound and determined to make New Jersey safe from teen drivers —which is probably a good thing. I still say a designated learner's lane with bumpers is not a bad idea.

If Eisenhower could create an entire interstate system, I don't see why we can't create an interstate bumper-car system. I'm just sayin.'

But while New Jersey legislators want teen drivers to place decals on their cars marking them as learners so the rest of us can take alternate routes on, say, Jupiter, I am wondering when someone is going to sit up and take notice of my proposal for safer highways — namely to create a computerized scrolling screen for cars that would let us know when drivers are listening to "YMCA."

It has never been proven but I'm sure DWYMCA (driving while "YMCA"-ing) has led to countless accidents. I know because I almost caused some of them.

Well?

Have you ever tried singing it without making the hand motions?

Don't get me wrong. It would certainly help to let people know they were driving behind a newly minted driver.

If New Jersey requires the giant "L" decal for "learner" we likely would afford those drivers more courtesy, meaning allowing them more space so they could hit somebody else's car if they miscalculate the turn.

But why stop there?

Perhaps drivers prone to putting on mascara while driving could put big "M" decals on their cars.

Drivers who balance their checkbooks while driving could, well, just have a big "S" for "stupid."

Obviously, pastors' cars should be clearly marked at all times so you know not to make obscene gestures. It is an unwritten rule that ministers from any denomination can drive as slowly as they want and no one can point any digits other then the index finger in their direction or use curse words outside their context in the Bible.

Maybe it wouldn't be such a bad idea if our boss' car were marked, too, so we don't arrive at work to learn this bit of trivia: she is an excellent lip reader.

My daughter Shannon soon will be a driver. Of course, I recently signed a legally binding contract which forbids me to write about her in this column lest she take me to court and win all the family assets, by which I mean the cats, so instead I will talk about one of her friends who is getting her license at about the same time.

Her name is, er, Thannon. Yeah, that's right, Thannon.

So, Thannon will be 16 in three months and her mother — who by the way is very attractive and intelligent — has been thinking of ways to keep Thannon from hitting other cars and other cars from hitting her.

To ensure Thannon's safety on the road, her mother — did I mention she also is stylish? — is considering the following steps:

- Purchasing her grandmother's 1985 Buick with only 15,000 miles on it. You can't get that kind of full metal jacket in a Hummer;
- Hiding the Disco Gold CD with "YMCA" on it;
- Ordering a specially made decal that says: Proud Daughter of an Uninsured, Unemployed Mother Who, Even If You Sue Her, Could Not Give You One Red Cent.

Other than that, Thannon likely will be coated in layers of bubble wrap whenever she leaves the house and have a curfew of, say, 8 p.m.

Or maybe it's time to just move to Jupiter.

Section 2

Thongs Get in Your Eye

And other hazards of life

Stupid guy tricks highlight differences in gender

Having a big brother teaches you early about the differences between males and females, important truths you will carry with you throughout life.

Since I was a kid and my big brother was knocked unconscious by a parked car, I knew guys would do anything to:

A) get an adrenaline rush;
B) get attention from girls;
C) not back down from a double-dog dare even it could potentially lead to, say, a concussion or loss of limb.

Guys have the philosophy: Act now, think later — and sometimes "later" means 20 or 30 years.

My brother's incident occurred when, after a rare snow, he was sledding down a steep hill in a parking lot on a trash can lid, which is known for their aerodynamics but not necessarily safety features such as power steering and airbags. This, as any female would know, makes undertaking this activity inherently dangerous, and therefore idiotic.

Losing control of the lid, my brother slid beneath a parked car, smacking his head on its underside at a great rate of speed.

He lived, but for a few days his head was pretty sore and I think he wiped out sixth grade, but it turns out he didn't need it anyway.

Among his friends, my brother was hailed a hero, a daredevil: the Evel Knievel of our cul-de-sac.

Men, I have learned, do not outgrow this.

Earlier this month in Vallejo, Calif., a guy was arrested for — remember, I would never lie to you — *punching a camel.*

The attack, according to the FoxNews.com report, was unprovoked.

The camel did not, for instance, offer to buy this guy's girlfriend a drink.

It did not throw down a challenge to his sports team.

As far as anyone can determine, the camel did not so much as insult the guy's driving.

Why, you are likely thinking if you are a woman, would a guy assault a perfectly innocent camel?

If you are a guy, you are thinking: "Cool," and then "Someone musta dared him."

According to the story, that's exactly what happened. On a dare from his closest friends, meaning guys who appreciate his ability to burp the National Anthem, the 24-year-old (*24!*) went into a restricted area of Six Flags Discovery Kingdom, cold-cocked the unsuspecting camel, whose last thought before blacking out, if it was female, was: "Why would a guy assault a perfectly innocent camel?" But a guy camel would have known and, on some level, understood. He may have thought, "Cool," before losing consciousness.

The attacker and the driver of the "getaway car" were arrested.

The women working in our newsroom, upon hearing this story, remarked that 24 seemed awfully old to be: making dares, taking dares and hanging out at theme parks with a bunch of guys getting arrested for assaulting camels.

I know better.

Last weekend, I accompanied a friend to a cookout. Two of the 30-something guys at the gathering — guys with good-paying jobs at a large engineering firm at which, we assume, they are required to actually think — decided to have a towel-snapping contest in which they popped twisted, wet towels at various body parts in an effort to inflict pain.

I know what you're thinking:

Women: "Why?"

Men: "Cool."

On the first pass, the *whip-snap* of the towel would have made Indiana Jones proud. The victim managed not to flinch despite the fact that a large welt appeared on the back of his leg and, I kid you not, began bleeding.

The contest continued despite the appearance of blood, which women respond to by securing the area and beginning first aid, and men respond to with: "Cool."

Soon, the guys were comparing towel marks in regions that are typically covered by clothing.

I have lived a great many years and I can say without hesitation that I have never witnessed two women snapping wet towels at each other, and the only time I have seen women draw blood was when only one designer purse was left on the 80 percent off table.

I also have never seen a woman go up to a guy and say, "Ooooh, the way you snap that towel really revs my engine. Wanna buy me a drink?"

What does this tell us about the differences between the genders?

A) Women do not inflict pain on themselves or others *unless* there are serious discounts involved, and
B) Men should spend more time thinking.

Also, if there are guys around, you might want to lock your linen closet and, just to be safe, keep your camel indoors.

GIRL studies Big-Texas-Cinnamon-Roll Incident

Poor blondes.

Everyone making all those jokes, entire books of them, and that was *before* Paris, Britney and Lindsay came along.

It's a darn shame.

It's not as if blondes are the only stupid females in the world.

In the interest of fairness and avoiding charges of discrimination, the topic of this week's report from the Gender Intelligence Research Lab (or GIRL) is why we women are forced to endure really stupid Ben Stiller movies and repeated displays of public male scratching of areas that would otherwise be considered private.

I am such a kidder. What I meant to say is, GIRL will study why females, on occasion, might, just possibly, do things considered by others as being gray-matter challenged.

We'll take this lesson in two parts:

1. Is the color of one's hair relevant if no one can prove its natural shade?

And, 2. Females may be ignorant but we ain't stupid.

Let's start with an example of the theory that one's brain activity decreases in direct proportion to the amount of dye on one's hair.

The subject of this example is a reporter in our newsroom we'll call Jean Cole (mainly because that's her name).

She is not a blonde but she plays one on TV.

Kidding again!

Seriously, Jean is a redhead, a talented copy editor and gifted writer, who is known around the newsroom for — how can we put this delicately? —being a safety hazard.

I am not sure, but I think Jean's mom coined the phrase: "You'll put your eye out!"

Not many people know this, but when safety goggles first were invented, they were called "Lenses to Keep Jean Cole from Putting Her Eye Out."

The inescapable fact is, we cannot leave Jean alone around construction sites, rogue rose bushes or hot-tempered Big Texas Cinnamon Rolls.

The reason is simple: No matter what Jean might be doing — editing, writing, saying "awwww" over pictures of cute kitties — her eye might suddenly suffer injury as if a bug with a serious case of Sky Rage just flew right in there on a suicide mission.

The time Jean did the most damage, hereinafter to be referred to as the Big Texas Cinnamon Roll Incident, or BTCRI, was a lesson in what can happen when you are so hungry you shove a vending machine pastry the size of a dinner plate in your mouth, causing the razor-sharp edge of the plastic wrapper to jam right into your cornea. (Why these wrappers weren't safety tested before they were unleashed on unsuspecting redheads is a question for another day).

The injury had barely healed when some debris from a construction site attached itself to Jean's left eye, causing one side of her face to swell and turn red, resembling a womp-sided, overripe tomato.

And then, days later, the recovering eye took a beating from a Rose of Sharon bush in Jean's yard that, as she described it, came at her "from outta nowhere."

Jean is now healed but all of us in the newsroom were stunned one day to discover the vending man had stocked our once harmless machine (if you don't count contributing to massive coronaries, obesity and sugar highs) with — cue ominous music — Big Texas Cinnamon Rolls.

We moved Jean's desk as far from the vending machine as possible and if someone does purchase a Big Texas Cinnamon Roll, he or she is asked to destroy the wrapper before entering the newsroom, which is a Big-Texas-Cinnamon-Roll-wrapper-free zone.

But it's unfair to let Jean stand alone in the battle of gender intelligence. And, really, she was the victim in the aforementioned incidences. It's not as if she *dared* the rose bush to attack her.

So here are other examples that prove females can, on some occasions, be as dumb as guys:

1. Two of them married Michael Jackson.

2. They cannot stop at merely dressing themselves. That limits the shopping options. Some women dress their little yappy dogs in cute outfits to make them even more annoying to the general public. I see this as dog abuse.

What if these misguided pet owners, and I hesitate to even think it, are *forcing their own fashion sensibilities onto their pets* and are therefore embarrassing them to the point that they no longer want to hump guests' legs or drink from the toilet?

What if Chico was a Bermuda-shorts-and-black-socks type of guy and his master is dressing him in a smoking jacket and ascot? Is this really fair to the dogs, and even if it is, is it fair to those of us who have to look at them?

And perhaps most telling of all:

3. A San Francisco woman, who has a medically recognized "objects fetish," claims she married the Eiffel Tower, according to a story published in April by the Telegraph in England. She has taken on the name of her husband and is now Erika La Tour Eiffel, not to be confused with her sister Betsy Berlin Wall.

Sure, Erika may seem a little nutty, but is she really *stupid?* I mean, she is one of the only women in recorded history to find a mate who won't argue or leave his underwear on the floor.

And — I'm going out on a limb here — I bet this is one spouse who will never, ever leave the toilet seat up.

A girls' guide
to safe thong-wearing

I feel I must apologize to my coworker, Jean "Safety Hazard" Cole, who was the subject of a recent column.

We in the newsroom thought Lean Jean the Eye-Injuring Machine, as we call her for short, was an anomaly, the only person in the world who could "shoot her eye out" with seemingly innocent objects such as a Big Texas Cinnamon Roll from the vending machine or a Rose of Sharon bush with a Clint Eastwood complex ("Do ya feel lucky, punk? Well do ya?")

I admit it. I was wrong.

On Monday, a Los Angeles woman filed a lawsuit claiming she has suffered a life-altering eye injury from — I hate to say it for fear of creating a nationwide underwear panic — a thong.

Yes, a pair of panties, which in my experience have always been non-violent, has joined the list of items mamas must warn children about: "You are not old enough for your own thong. You could put your eye out." Or in an argument with a teen daughter: "I don't care what your friends are doing. I'd rather see you with visible panty lines than lying in an emergency room somewhere."

And this does make a good cautionary tale for mothers of teen boys who can warn their sons of the dangers of getting anywhere near girls' underwear.

According to the Associated Press, the injured 52-year-old woman is suing Victoria's Secret, claiming a pair of its Sexy Little Thing low-rise v-strings is defective.

The woman claims a "decorative metallic piece" flew off the undies, striking her in the eye and damaging her cornea. The injury cost her a few days' missed work and will be "affecting her the rest of her life," according to thesmokinggun.com. No monetary amount was listed for damages, other than a check in the box for "Action is an unlimited civil case (amount exceeds $25,000)", which in lawyer speak means "the amount a large company is willing to give to make the problem disappear."

You, like me, may be envisioning the woman stretching the underwear, slingshot-like, between her left forefinger and right thumb, readying it for a shot at the head of her significant other who likely gave the wrong answer to "Does this make my butt look big?" Suddenly, the thong goes awry, as thongs are wont to do, and life as she knows it is over.

But, alas, that is not what occurred. The "victim," it seems, can take no part of the blame for the errant thong. Her suit states that at the time of the injury the product was "being used in the manner intended" and "in a manner that was readily foreseeable by defendants as involving a substantial danger not readily apparent. Adequate warnings of danger were not given."

Hmmm. If I read the legal-eze correctly, the suit is saying Victoria's Secret should have been aware the thong had mayhem on its mind, even though it gave no signs, and should have put a warning on the label.

Perhaps Sexy Little Things should come with instructions for safe use:
Upon stepping from shower, follow these steps:

1. Don safety goggles and helmet. Steel-toed boots are not required but are recommended.
2. Grasp v-string with left thumb at Point A and right thumb at Point B, as shown in diagram. Hold thumbs apart, spreading elasticized strings of garment to approximate width of user's hips.
3. Gingerly place Foot 1, the right, into Space C. Once it is firmly on the floor, repeat process with Foot 2, the left, and Space D.
4. Carefully tug garment at Points E and F until it comes to rest securely on Pelvis, marked P.
    Note: *Do not* remove safety equipment until garment has been safely covered by outer garment such as a skirt, jeans or other form of slacks. In fact, skirts should be avoided because, while user's eyes are now safe, others could be struck by flying decorative metallic objects if user abruptly crosses her legs or walks across a subway grate.

I asked Jean, who is familiar with corneal injuries, her thoughts on the subject. She thinks this is one eye injury she could have avoided.

"If I was a 52-year-old woman and I was putting on a thong, I would've had my eyes closed," she said.

Now there's some good safety advice.

Movies for guys
get dumb and dumber

After I wrote a column questioning why guys pay to see increasingly dumb and dumber movies, a female coworker said if I published it, I'd likely never date again.

She'll need a better threat than that, since I wouldn't remember what a date looked like if one arrived at my door with flowers, chocolates and a nametag that read, "Hi, I'm your date." (Besides, I always have trouble reading when someone is holding chocolate in front of me).

A male coworker said the column was "a little harsh" and maybe it would work better in a women's magazine (i.e., stick it where no male would ever see it). Then he added, "I'm not saying what you wrote isn't true."

I figure guys are smart enough (see, I'm giving the idio...er, guys, some credit) to decide if what I write applies to them, and if it doesn't, to not get their Hanes in a twist.

What I pondered in the column is this: Why would a perfectly normal-seeming man waste 102 minutes and a $10 box of popcorn on a movie called "Balls of Fury" (substitute "Dodgeball" or "Ace Ventura: Pet Detective")?

The answer, as I discovered during New Year's week when my dad was staying at our typically girls-only house, is that men's brains have been numbed by the drivel sportscasters impart on television. After many years of viewing sporting events, their judgment is permanently impaired.

Over the course of eight college football bowl games – which is about, I'd say, eight more than my daughter Shannon and I would typically watch – I heard many comments that tested the theory that sportscasters are smarter than your average sweaty locker room towel, including, "Does that Astroturf look like it needs mowing to you?" and "Speaking from the point of view of an ex-lineman who was hit in the head many, many times, I'd have to say: the team that gets the most points will win this game tonight."

Minds suitably numbed from the stimulating analysis – enough to hold until baseball season – men could now watch movies featuring scenes of heavy cleavage, bodily function humor and other men being hit in the crotch with a variety of blunt instruments (or sometimes by their on-screen love interests).

It's a genre of films I like to call Stupid Guy Movies Featuring Heavy Cleavage, Bodily Function Humor and Crotch Shots.

Researchers discovered after a test that likely involved sitting through a 24-hour marathon of "Dumb and Dumber" that men like slapstick, while women are emotionally fulfilled by films featuring intelligent humor (Some men refer to these as "chick flicks." I call them movies in which you won't find a former stand-up comedian playing all the characters, including those of a large black woman and the leading stud).

Say it with me now, girls: "duh-huh."

This is why you don't see women driving cars with bumper stickers that say "I (heart) passing gas" and forming fan clubs for The Three Stooges.

One researcher found that slapstick is popular among men because 1) they are competitive and therefore feel better about themselves when others seem stupider than they are, and 2) they don't mind seeing others in pain, while women avoid displays of physical discomfort.

I know what you're thinking: There are those women who like nothing better than watching another woman's pain, otherwise how would you explain the popularity of shows like "Bridezilla," or the whole can't-get-enough-of-the-train-wreck-that-is-Britney's-life phenomenon?

And the gender lines may continue to blur. Recently, two women in the newsroom visited a Web site called farts.com and proceeded to laugh until they were making questionable noises themselves.

But there are some lines I won't cross – if I ever do go on another date, I refuse to see any movie with "ball" in the title or starring Ben Stiller, Adam Sandler or Will Ferrell. Unless, maybe, there are Milk Duds involved.

Sometimes, Luvey's all you need

It should come as no surprise to anyone that the creator of the modern Valentine's Day was a woman.

It may be more surprising, though, that she never married. No, Esther Howland died single but rich from the money that poured into her father's stationery store after she cleverly thought of mass-producing Valentine's cards in 1847.

Esther would likely have been proud to learn that the tired, the alone, the unbethrothed masses have created Single Awareness Day as an alternative to the sweet, pink togetherness that abounds on Feb. 14. This gives people a reason to call out "Happy SAD" to other loners. Apparently, this brings a smile to their faces, although the cutesy phrase makes me about as sick as one of those side-burned gorillas that sings "Love Me Tender" when you push a part of its plush anatomy that, trust me, you would not poke if it were real.

As of yet, no one has created a Happy SAD greeting card, but give it time. The purpose of the holiday, after all, is sales. Oh, and giving men a way to get out of whatever doghouse they've crawled into and women an excuse to substitute chocolate for that ever-present, low-cal drinkable lunch.

I know what you're thinking. As a single mom, I am suffering from sour grapes (or wilted flowers, or unfermented wine...whatever).

Really, I have nothing against Valentine's Day, and just so you know, I did have plans Thursday night: I lit a roaring, romantic fire in the fireplace and slithered into a low-cut satin top. Then I vacuumed and washed two loads of laundry. After that, I sang, "Luvey's all you need" (think Beatles tune) to my cat Luvey and ate chocolate I purchased myself until I felt sick enough to go to bed early and watch old musicals on Turner Classic Movies. It doesn't get any better than that.

It just seems that setting aside one day each year to treat your loved one in a special way is along the same lines as having to ask a man to tell you he loves you or buying your own engagement ring.

And it is a little odd that the same holiday celebrated by some with a Spider-Man card that reads, "I'm in a tangle over you" is observed by others with a gift of a red-lace, thong teddy.

I'm just sayin.'

The paradoxical holiday also can turn dark for women expecting to get a call from a certain someone who, it turns out, stayed home to watch the game on his 60-inch flat screen which, it turns out, he loves enough to list as his next of kin. And then there are those men who were not in the doghouse pre-Valentine's but who wind up there simply because love, to them, was exemplified by a set of can-slicing, hammer-impervious Ronco steak knives.

With all this confusion, it's no wonder the new Valentine's motto is "Happy SAD."

Maybe, next year, we should all spend the night singing to our cats and watching musicals. Give me a call and together we'll ignore Valentine's Day — unless some hot guy calls and asks me to dinner at Dolce.

I'm just sayin.'

Meet my daughter,
Touch-Me-and-You-Die

Moms heed this warning: Never, ever wait until you are in the throes of severe labor pains and the fog of heavy narcotics before choosing a baby name.

It's during this time that moms have been known to become angry at someone: the doctor for not getting the baby out fast enough, the nurse who refused to let her drink water, the mother-in-law who keeps smiling and yammering about the joys of motherhood, her husband for getting her into the situation, her husband for smiling and yammering about the joys of motherhood, her husband because he didn't gain 40 pounds, and, yes, perhaps even the tiny, innocent baby who, I must point out, did not ask to be there.

But the combination of narcotics and anger can be the only explanations for the name a New Zealand mom saddled her daughter with: Talula Does the Hula From Hawaii.

It's a matter of court record. Would I lie to y'all?

A New Zealand judge, who was handling the case in which Talula Does the Hula From Hawaii's parents split and were fighting for her custody, decided the parents had psychologically damaged the 9-year-old, who told classmates her name was "K" to avoid teasing. The judge, expressing his displeasure over the rash of strange names for babies, made Talula Does the Hula From Hawaii (I just like the sound of it) a ward of the court so she could change her name.

Maybe Talula Does the Hula From Hawaii (last time, I promise) will become "Ann" or "Mary."

Apparently, registrars in New Zealand can refuse to record some requested names, such as Fish and Chips, Yeah Detroit, Stallion, Twisty Poi, Keenan Got Lucy and Sex Fruit.

Shame. I would've liked to meet Sex Fruit.

But names that got past the registrars include Number 16 Bus Shelter, Midnight Chardonnay and Violence.

Let's see: "Number 16 Bus Shelter?" This child's parents likely were celebrating the site of conception, which gives us a good reason to avoid public transportation when visiting New Zealand.

"Midnight Chardonnay?" Only two occupations await her: stripper-slash-porn star or soap opera actress. Not that there's anything *wrong* with that. It's good to have choices.

"Violence?" Clearly, these parents are hoping for a rapper who makes enough coin that they can trade their hoopty ride for a tricked-out Benz wagon.

But if the judge thinks this trend is occurring only in New Zealand, he hasn't been watching Entertainment Tonight.

Everyone thought Michael Jackson naming his child Blanket was a sign of the same mind-eating illness that turned his skin white and caused his nose to fall off but in reality, he was a trendsetter. It wasn't long before actor Jason Lee named his son Pilot Inspecktor, magician Penn Jillette named his daughter Moxie Crimefighter, reality star Rooster McConaughey (brother of Matthew) named his son Miller Lyte and actor Rob Morrow named his son Tu (read the names together.)

Obviously, celebrities have a motive for their cruelty: A few mentions in the press and another two minutes of fame at the expense of their kids' wellbeing and their ability to attract mates later in life.

Earlier this month, a dad in Orlando, Fla., offered the right to name his unborn son to DJs at a local radio station who were offering a $100 gas card to the listener who came up with the most interesting item to trade. Radio hosts Richard Dixon and J. Willoughby took David Partin up on his offer and named the boy, due this winter, "Dixon And Willoughby Partin."

While free gas almost qualifies as a legitimate reason to give your baby a name that will scar him for life, I see this trend as child abuse.

Babies ought to be assigned letters or numbers until they are old enough to choose their own names, say around age 4.

Then, we'd see kids named Spider-Man Smith, Barbie's Dream House Johnson, Puddin' Pop Wilson or Wii's Guitar Hero Hudson but at least *they* made the choice.

Or, we could wait until the age of 14 and let parents decide. That way we'd have something to hang over their heads during those teen years when they're going to hate us anyway.

As the mom of a teenage daughter, I can think of a few examples for girls: Chastity Belt, Pretty Prude, or Touch Me And You Die.

Or threaten to name a son Dirty Underwear Harry.

Hey, it's only fair. He's the one who insisted on embarrassing you by wearing his pants around his knees, piercing his tongue and dating someone named Talula Does the Hula From Hawaii (oops. That one slipped out).

On the plus side, he might actually wear *clean* underwear, just to spite you.

Well, officer, sometimes stupid *is* an emergency

It was only a matter of time before someone snapped.

Of all the things that can make a person crazy, getting home with a bag of fast food and discovering your special sauce is missing ranks right up there with starting to pull into the last empty parking space and seeing a motorcycle tucked into one tiny corner of it.

It's a wonder we haven't all shaved our heads from sheer madness.

But, after all, that's why God gave us impulse control. Most of us, anyway.

Just as we learn at around age 2 not to wet our pants in public — most of us, anyway — we reach a certain age where we know not to bludgeon drivers who cut us off in traffic, poison our neighbor's prize roses because her dog pooped in our yard or step from a limo wearing a microscopic skirt and no underwear.

But there comes a time in every person's life when he reaches his limit, when he can no longer hold back the stupid.

That's when he calls for backup.

Last week, a Jacksonville, Fla., man unleashed his stupid on an unsuspecting public after he discovered someone left the sauce off his spicy Italian Subway sandwich. Of course he did what any red-necked American nutcase would do — he dialed 911 to let deputies at the Jacksonville Sheriff's Office know the severity of the problem and to request they ensure his order was made to his specifications, according to Associated Press reports.

But the man's displeasure extended beyond the service at Subway. He dialed 911 again to ask what was taking deputies so long to arrive. Sheesh. Here our public servants were making this poor guy wait for a resolution to his sauce emergency while they were out investigating some kidnapping or robbery or something.

What is this world coming to?

When deputies finally did arrive, they attempted to tell the disbelieving man there was no such thing as a Sauce SWAT Team. They finally were forced to arrest him, charging him with making false 911 calls.

I'm not sure, but I'm guessing court fees will cost more than a "five-dolla foot long."

Maybe we shouldn't be so hard on the guy. Is there any one of us who hasn't wanted to have authorities enforce our fast food order? Wouldn't we all like to hear a mirror-Ray-Banned officer say to the teen in the drive-through: "Go ahead, punk, make my day. Are ya gonna forget the lady's onion rings again? Well are ya?"

And who hasn't considered calling reinforcements to Taser the neighborhood kid who creates a 7.4 quake at 2 a.m. when he rides through the cul-de-sac with his stereo booming?

Wouldn't we all like to have someone with cuffs handy when a woman cuts in front of us in line while back-to-school shopping at a store whose air conditioner had failed and everyone was hot and sweaty and all the employees were on break but one? Not that I'm speaking from personal experience.

Isn't that why we pay tax dollars? To have someone protect our rights?

But perhaps the money would be better spent to protect people from themselves. Maybe the government could create an Idiocy Task Force to arrest really stupid people when they cross the line into lunacy or our air space.

Nah. I guess that's not realistic.

The officers would have to spend way too much time in Hollywood trying to get stars to put on underwear. Plus, there's not enough jail space for the people who make those really bad reality shows.

I'm just sayin.'

The only thing to fear is... teenagers

I have tasted fear.

It tasted a little like a breakfast burrito backing up on me but that's not the point.

The point is that everyone has fears but I'm not sure mine count as real, medically recognized phobias.

For instance, I feel sweaty pricks of panic every time I let my daughter get in the car with a teenage boy.

And I am overcome with cold, clammy anxiety until the moment I open her cell phone bill, at which point I sink to the ground, overcome by nausea.

But I don't have a fear with a name, like the fear of spiders (arachnophobia) that my daughter has. When she sees an eight-legged creature in her bathtub, she screams, "Mom! Come quick! Get the spider."

I come running and then she says, "Don't hurt it!"

The reason I am not afraid of spiders is because I could squash them like, well, bugs. See, I am *lots* bigger than the majority of spiders, though some of those Amazonian ones I've seen on the Discovery Channel — the ones that look like they could be saddled and ridden to herd cattle— might give me a run for my money.

I figure that even if the spider is sitting in the bathtub, three or four legs raised in a threatening manner, shouting, "You want a piece of me?" I can say, "Yeah," and pull off one of its legs.

Instead, I'll put the spider in a jar and release it in the yard where it can go home to its spider wife and children and say, "You should have seen it. I had her right where I wanted her."

Even spiders deserve to maintain some dignity.

Shannon's fear of spiders does not keep her from functioning as a normal teen, although she avoids horror movies involving spiders, going into our garage, and cleaning the Skittles-encrusted corners of her bedroom (though I suspect this last one is due to perspirophobia, or fear of doing actual sweating).

Some people, though, have fears that are downright debilitating.

How, for instance, do you marry or hold a job when you have a fear of chins (geniophobia)? When you have a baby, do you cover his chin in little blue bandages? Are all the framed photos in the house of faces from the nose up?

Other fears that might prevent someone from living normally include: fear of knees (genuphobia), fear of gravity (barophobia) and fear of oneself (autophobia).

These are real, diagnosed afflictions. (Would I lie to you?)

The person who has linonophobia, or fear of string, likely had a big brother like mine who rigged some dowels and string to the light switch in our windowless bathroom when I was a child so that when I closed the door I was trapped in total darkness, left until I was a whimpering puddle and rescued hours later by my mommy. Not that I have a fear of the dark (scotophobia).

And people with levophobia, fear of things to the left side of the body, must have found themselves sitting in the window seat on a 13-hour plane ride sitting to the right of Dr. Phil.

Some fears seem plausible to me to the point that I wonder why they are considered debilitating.

- Fear of work (ergophobia). All journalists suffer from this. It's why we have careers in which writing about a tomato with a growth that could best be described as pornographic is called work.
- Fear of missiles or bullets (ballistophobia). I've never seen anyone run *toward* a bullet, except maybe Superman and Donald Trump (that hair helmet could withstand anything).
- Fear of the great mole rat (zemmiphobia). It's likely I would not be afraid of a common house *mole rat*. But a *great* mole rat? Isn't everybody?

The most realistic fear on the list is ephebiphobia, or fear of teenagers. Sure, I've survived two years with one but I have four to go. Each day it becomes more difficult to breathe without using a paper bag.

If I were to name real phobias that haunt parents of teens, they would be:

- Interruptophobia, fear of finally, after 10 years, having five minutes alone in a hot bath and having someone burst in and shout, "Mom, have you seen my other blue soccer sock? Oh, and I need a ride to the field. In five minutes."
- Lowfundophobia, fear of running out of money before they move out.
- Bottomlesspitophobia, fear of never being able to fill them up.
- I'mtoooldtoraiseanotherbaby!ophobia, fear of becoming a grandparent.

On second thought, maybe I do have a phobia, one called pantophobia, which is not a fear of polyester slacks like one might think.

No, it's a fear of everything, which I'll likely have until my teen grows up and has her own kids. Then I'll give it to her.

Nude maid strips man
of self respect

A story appeared in the news this week that once again highlights the differences in genders.

I feel it is part of my role as a respected and not-so-highly paid journalist to continue research into the age-old question of whether males or females are smarter.

So far, women have supported my efforts. Guys, well, they haven't sent too much hate mail (oh, and to the guy named Mark who responded negatively to my previous column about stupid guy tricks: The word "video" does not have two 'I's. Ever.)

I'm not saying one gender is smarter than the other. That would be unethical.

I report. You decide.

What follows is my latest example of gender differences: A Florida man hired a woman, for $100 per hour according to CNN, to clean his house while his wife was out of town.

Was he doing his wife a favor?

Did he want her to be surprised to come home to a sparkling clean house?

Did he realize she would treasure this more than any welcome-home seduction he might plan?

I know what you women are thinking: "Wow, I wish my husband were more like him."

You won't be thinking that for long.

As it turns out, the husband wasn't paying such a steep price to have someone buff the floors — he was paying her to clean *in* the buff.

So now female readers may be thinking he's not such a great guy after all.

But wait! There's more.

While the man wasn't looking, the naked maid, whom we'll call Dust Bunny, allegedly stole $40,000 in jewelry that belonged to the man's wife.

Now the wife, when she comes home or goes online or picks up any newspaper in the nation, is likely going to be furious or highly embarrassed (I'm guessing both) that her husband hires nude maids *and* she doesn't even have her diamonds to comfort her.

All the women say it with me: Bless her heart.

Guys, at this point, have likely picked up on the more obvious (to guys) mystery in this whole incident: Where does a naked woman put $40,000 in jewelry...?

(Pause while we all ponder this.)

...*and* if this man was paying $100 per hour to have a naked woman in his house, why wasn't he watching her?

I imagine to some, this would seem wasteful.

What does this man have left?

He has been stripped, so to speak, of his pride, the jewelry, a hundred bucks per hour and any guy-type respect he may have earned for hiring a naked maid in the first place.

I'm just sayin'.

Men in tights? They'll learn

I wasn't too upset when men went all metrosexual and got in touch with their feminine sides.

No right-minded woman is going to turn away a man who smells nice and wears clean shirts, which, she can only hope, are qualities that extend to his undergarments. And it's always nice to be able to gaze up at your man and see past the nose hair to his eyes.

Even men using lotions and cream rinses didn't seem so bad, though I was starting to get nervous when so many guys began getting their hair highlighted.

It seemed a little competitive, if you ask me.

I managed not to fret when I saw men who could beat me in a Miss Maid of Cotton pageant, calmly reminding myself that, while they may be prettier, they're still prone to scratching their nether regions in public and beginning conversations with, "Pull my finger."

Now, just when I thought men had gotten tired of playing dress up, when I could walk down the street holding my head high without fearing some porcelain-skinned, Titanic-era Leo DiCaprio might walk past and show me up, some goober goes and invents male makeup.

I'm not talking Johnny-Depp-as-a-pirate makeup; I'm talking everyday makeup geared toward your average soccer dad. Some products include Manscara and Guyliner, names as adorable as the men who wear them.

And — you know I never kid you — several online businesses are selling male pantyhose and tights. Men have even formed a group called e-MANcipate in support of male hosiery, whose Web site at www.e-mancipate.net includes this headline: "Truck driver tells of wearing pantyhose during long trips."

It's times like these when I say to myself, "Self, you are looking mighty cute today."

After a thank you and a brief discussion of where I bought my blouse, I get back on subject and say to myself: "Men must be nuttier than Aunt Ella Dean's fruitcake and twice as rum-soaked."

What clear-thinking man would choose to wear makeup and pantyhose?

Everyone knows these were forms of torture created by men to keep women subservient.

Cro-Magnon Man knew his woman couldn't easily escape the cave, whose floor by the way was strewn with his dirty loincloths, if she were wearing control tops, especially when they got all tangled up in her leg fur.

And Medieval men knew women couldn't rise up in battle if they had to keep checking their lip gloss in the armor of the knight standing next to them.

The only reason women are still tied to these age-old conventions is because no woman wants to be the first to arrive at the church social or Bunko night with bare-naked eyebrows and legs pale enough to make the children cry.

If only one of us could break free, we'd all be liberated.

So if guys want to highlight their hair, paint their faces and wrestle themselves into pantyhose before work each morning, I say let them.

When enough of them get hooked, maybe we women will find the courage to break free of our chains and then we'll rule the world.

Oh, that's right, we already do.

Then we'll have to shoot for controlling the remote.

New teen repellent has practical uses

Tired of those biting, stinging pests?

Getting a headache from those annoying buzzing and chirping noises?

Looking for a cure for that ever-present pain in your neck?

An English company hopes to solve your problems with its new invention that scatters society's biggest pests: teens. (Hey, I'm not the one who said it. It's in the brochure. OK, fine. I *was* thinking it.)

Apparently, the U.S. is not the only country where teens congregate on street corners and in business parking lots, making noise, harassing potential customers and generally acting as if they are on some sort of psychedelic hormone trip. So the British company Kids Be Gone developed the Mosquito Ultrasonic Teen Deterrent, and, no, this is not taken from the plot of a sci-fi movie featuring a planet on which only adults are allowed to live.

This is a real-for-sure, hi-tech gadget reviewed by The Wall Street Journal. You have to believe something written right next to an article headlined: "16 hot dividend stocks."

The gadget takes advantage of the fact that we oldsters (anyone over the age of 20) have such damaged hearing that we can't detect the sounds it emits. But apparently to those under 20, the high-decibel noise is painful and, according to one advertisement, can scatter an entire spray-paint-wielding gang in under four minutes.

Momentarily, this made me smile. Members of aforementioned spray-paint-wielding gang are likely the ones who caused our hearing loss in the first place by vibrating — without our permission — eardrums, cars, homes, streets and entire neighborhoods with enough bass to shatter glass.

Gangstas, meet karma.

Then I hesitated. Lots of those pesky kids hanging out at businesses spend more money than their parents, drive nicer cars and have better credit records.

Business owners might want to rethink scaring off one of the largest segments of the buying public, not to mention the havoc the high sounds might cause among neighborhood dogs and babies.

Still, the Mosquito could have practical uses.

Keep it handy when your daughter's first date comes to the door. If he has a tricked-out Volkswagon van with shag carpet on the walls, don't hesitate: Repel him.

Take it on road trips for easy use when your 10-year-old starts giving the 7-year-old Indian burns or holding a finger an inch from her face and chanting, "I'm not touching you, I'm not touching you."

Keep inside the front door so it's ready when you come home early from a weekend getaway to find 30 teens who don't belong to you, a keg of beer iced down in your bathtub, a couple making out in the closet and a pizza upside down on your new white sofa.

While this invention would be handy for any parent, I'm thinking of investing in another hi-tech repellent. Developed by MIT's Media Lab, the No-Contact Jacket sends a jolt to those who invade your personal space.

This would have been great to have when I was in high school and we had this guy in our class who was incapable of greeting a female without touching some part of her anatomy, unable to comprehend that those parts are covered by clothing for a reason. That might have been OK if he'd looked like Brad Pitt but he was more, well, sweaty pits.

I could have pushed a button hidden at the hem of my sleeve and "ZAP!" — the ends of his hair would be singed and smoke would be coming from his ears.

Well, maybe that's only an Ally-McBeal-type fantasy. In reality, only a "small" electric shock is emitted.

Still, this is a tool women the world over have been needing for some time. It would be perfect for those darkened parking garages, singles bars and the office Christmas party.

Plus, we'd finally have the advantage when diving past the kids for the last chocolate chip cookie.

What? Like you're above a little harmless kid zapping if it means getting your chocolate fix?

Didn't think so.

It's a nice day
for a green wedding

Forget white weddings (no one's foolin' anyone, anyway).

Green weddings are in vogue. The British company Climate Care estimates a single wedding emits 14.5 tons of carbon dioxide, meaning the Holmes-Cruise extravaganza likely emitted enough gas to melt Donald Trump's combover.

But those Hollywood types who drive electric Matchbox cars and eat tofu caviar, which as we all know can be recycled into tractor tires or leisure suits, have not apparently realized the dangers of wedding excess (and by excess I mean events at which the bride and groom are not wearing Coors T-shirts and guests are not treated to Spam sandwiches).

According to a wedding planner for Plan It Green in Baltimore, even being beautiful on your wedding day can be hazardous. She recommends not using *any* aerosol hairspray. This advice will not be popular here in the South. There are two days in the life of a Southern woman when her hair requires a shellacking with Aqua Net that can withstand hurricane-force winds *and* a feuding family — her wedding and her funeral.

But, no, the planner continues, members of the wedding party should use organic hair care products. Maybe Dippity-do makes a line of tofu gels.

Prospective brides and grooms also should, the planner says, send recyclable invitations, hire musicians with acoustic instruments and serve organic spirits (i.e. wine that tastes like flat Co-Cola and gets you about as drunk.)

Here's my solution to the invitation problem: Print two — one for the scrapbook and one to send to your grandma who doesn't have a computer — and send e-mail to remaining guests. I know this likely will come as a shock

71

to those who just ordered $600 invitations and spent another $200 to have them addressed in calligraphy, but people *throw them away* as soon as they've read them, unless the recipient's a guy and he throws his away *before* he's finished reading.

I wonder why I haven't heard about this green wedding phenomenon on that TV show Bridezilla. I don't recall seeing an episode featuring a lovely young bride, wearing cowboy boots beneath a dress chosen to showcase the tattoo of Route 66 on her back, arguing with her mother, "It's My Special Day and I'll save some xo#@! trees if I want to."

I, for one, am all for simple weddings. I've heard enough of this "It's my special day" hooie. No one can even say, "You only get married once" with a straight face.

Especially those Bridezillas. Let's face it, if you pulled a gun on your maid of honor for ordering pink rather than peach roses, it doesn't bode well for the first time hubby throws his dirty underwear on the floor.

Think about it: Do guests really need keepsake beer mugs personalized with your initials?

And don't kid yourself. No one's ever going to wear that $40 "I'm the bridesmaid" T-shirt outside of your rehearsal.

The average wedding, according to Conde Nast Bridal Group, costs $27,852, more than some people make in a year.

Those Hollywood types spend more like $27 million, which does seem a tad hypocritical. Think of how many sessions of couples' counseling all those millions would buy — and all the trees that would be saved if they didn't have to print that 200-page divorce decree 72 hours after the wedding.

Maybe all people need is to be reminded that the focus should be the marriage rather than a half-hour wedding ceremony.

Because if there's one thing we need to *stop* recycling, it's spouses. They don't even make good leisure suits.

Relaxing nakation
will melt away worries

If it weren't for the extra pound or 30 I'm carrying around, I might just consider taking a nakation this year.

Never heard of one?

It's a vacation, only without clothes.

You'd be nekkid.

Don't get your drawers in a panic (if you're wearing any). Everyone else would be nekkid, too.

Seems nakations are all the rage these days. CNN — Curmudgeon News Network — said so. The reporter gives this quote: "'… there's the idea that if you've lost the shirt off your back, you should go nude,' said Erich Schuttauf, executive director of the American Association of Nude Recreation."

Director of nude recreation. Who knew?

I thought that was Hugh Hefner, who lost the shirt off his back years ago and has to go around wearing PJs.

Any-hoo, I think we Americans are more practical than Schuttauf thinks.

Basically, on a nakation:

- We don't have to worry what to pack: Sunscreen, shoes. Oh, and maybe a towel for those really hot car seats.
- We don't have to answer calls from the office because there's no place to carry our cell phones.
- We don't have to fix our hair or put on our makeup because no one will be looking at our faces.

I'm just sayin.'

Just a tip, though. Try taking a nakation to Disney World and you're likely to end up in a jail cell holding your Mickey Mouse ears over your nether regions.

But never fear. The CNN article recommended some resorts at which taking a nakation is not a felony.

Some, like the one in Kissimme, Fla., near Orlando, sound sunny and warm.

Others destinations had me befuddled, like Worley, Idaho, or Union City, Mich.

Really. Michigan?

They're going to put a nudist resort in a place where people wear longhandles on their wedding nights?

Sounds like someone stayed a little too long at the naked cookout without a hat and got brain frostbite.

But in toasty warm Wilton, Calif., the Laguna Del Sol resort hosts NudeStock each year, which I assume means you get to listen to really loud rock music, roll in the mud and relieve yourselves in Porta Potties, all while nekkid.

That's my kind of nakation.

Then there's the Avalon resort in the Nakation Capital of the World: PawPaw, W. Va. The Avalon hosts a Nude Year's Eve gala each year which leaves me wondering: What does one wear to such an event?

Avalon's Web site says men wear cummerbunds and bow ties but what about women? We like to feel special on New Year's Eve. It's not like I'm going to wear this same old skin that everyone's already seen me in. Besides, it's wrinkled and faded.

Maybe the women could wear tiaras.

But then there would be a fight over seeing another woman wearing the same thing as you.

I sure would hate to see the police have to come bust up a nude catfight between middle-aged women.

Oh, come on. Stop giggling.

It's so immature.

Everyone knows a 10 beats a zero every time

News flash: That gangly stage where girls are all elbows and knees with no strategically placed fleshy areas is not the prettiest phase of development. But for years, fashion designers told the public that clothes look best on models who look as if they are in the most awkward stage of adolescence, who look like wooden, waist-less mannequins rather than women.

Now we regular-sized women can rejoice — officials in Madrid made history by requiring models at a recent fashion event to have what organizers considered a healthy body mass index to participate.

It's a development I thought I'd never see in my lifetime — skinny women being turned away at the door after being weighed and checked and found, well, lacking.

It makes me want to jump for joy, but I'm way too mature for that (besides, the resulting breeze might knock over some of the models).

The fashion industry may be realizing what some advertising executives learned in the last year or so, that women do not have to be size 0 (the average size of today's fashion models) to sell clothes — or bath products or household cleansers — to size-14 women.

Dove's advertising campaign showing women of varying shapes, sizes and colors has been successful in selling us lotions and soaps.

Now, we might begin to see such women selling us clothes, which, if you think about it, is an idea too long in coming.

How many of us have ever seen one of those stick-figure runway models with smudged eyeliner, blue-streaked hair that desperately needs a brush and a funky one-sleeved blouse and thought "I want to look just like her?"

Not many women want to go to the grocery store looking like they're on their way to a convention for bulimic Star Trek fans.

And, in any case, I don't have shoulders that resemble a Rwandan child's and cheeks sunken enough to be an extra in a zombie movie.

Instead, I am a victim like most of you, a woman who sees an item of clothing on a catalog model and thinks, "How cute!" Then, after trying it on, realizes it is cute only in one size — if you can count zero as a size (or maybe it's referring to the daily caloric intake of the model).

It's like fashion designers have hidden cameras in dressing rooms so they can say "Gotcha!" when their sleek lines don't fall naturally over our curves and they have a good laugh at our expense.

I think women would be more likely to buy an item of clothing if they can see it looks good on someone their size — someone whose body has rounded out a bit since age 12.

So, I raise my Twinkie to you, Madrid officials, for underscoring a message the fashion industry should have figured out in middle school like the rest of us: Nobody wants to be a zero.

Run, girls:
Guys heading back to the cave

You might not think cavemen would inspire imitation, what with having to carry those heavy clubs and continually braid the hair on their knuckles to keep it from dragging the ground.

But the Geico cavemen must be having more of an impact on society than simply combining selling insurance with an odd-but-touching statement about stereotyping.

Men by the dozens are finding the solution to their quest for complete manliness in the commercials' missing links, especially now that the three-piece suited, modernly sensitive Neanderthals will star in a TV series on ABC this fall.

In a new trend, men are requesting plastic surgery to transplant hair follicles from their scalps to their chests, faces and bellies, according to an article in Newsweek.

If I'd read this in National Enquirer, I would have written off the trend as just another 80-pound newborn or two-headed boy raised by wolves.

But this was Newsweek. It says "news" right in its name.

The article states a contingency of men are growing tired of those mamby-pamby metrosexuals who are prettier, smell better and have smoother legs than the women they date.

This new breed of chest-pounding cavemanly men are labeled, in a perfect twist, retrosexuals.

Some men are even requesting squarer chins, angular jaws and larger noses.

It's just like men to get all emotional and overreact.

We need a woman to inject some logic and level-headedness to this situation.

I volunteer.

Guys, speaking for the vast majority of women (based on a non-scientific poll of Women Who Know What They're Talking About): Don't add any more hair to your backs and stomachs.

You may think you feel more manly. We think you feel like a damp bathmat.

We're not staring because we think you're hot.

Yes, the metros may have gone too far — tweezing and moisturizing are our turf and there's only so much room in front of the bathroom mirror. I'm glad the retros are taking a stand against chest-waxing and it would thrill me to date a guy who says, "You look beautiful tonight," instead of, "A pair of red, peep-toe heels would really make that outfit *pop!*"

But can't we find some equilibrium here? Haven't guys been walking upright long enough to find balance?

We can learn from the cavemen — stick with what God gave you. You didn't find Grog and Ock visiting Dr. Cro Magnon's office to request forehead reductions or brain implants.

They were secure in their prehistoric Homosapienness.

Women would put up with a lot to find a guy with that kind of confidence, even a naturally occurring hairy back.

Just don't opt for the knuckle-hair transplant — that's a deal-killer.

Commercials can make you sick

Back in the day, people knew they needed to see a doctor if they relied on the ache in their knees to predict rain or if they discovered something on their bodies that wasn't there the day before.

The something-ain't-right-here method stood people in good stead for centuries.

If Aunt Ida was a little concerned about a growth on her lip, she might ask Uncle Odell, "You think there's s'posed to be a hair growing from it?"

Depending on how he answered, and whether or not Grandma Eathel had a home remedy for hairy growths, she might call over to the doctor's office and he'd send over an ointment with instructions to "apply once daily." Aunt Ida'd never even ask what it was called, much less what it treated.

These days, though, everyone seems to have a medical degree. How do I know? I watch a lot of TV, where you'll find people like Fred and Bill, two ordinary guys chatting on the golf course. Fred — hair coiffed, ensemble coordinated, teeth bright enough for night hunting — will say to Bill: "Great shot! Those severe seasonal allergies must not be bothering you today."

Bill, grinning and slapping Fred on the back, will say: "I took the new prescription Fabu-Phen, Fred. It's fast acting and non drowsy. Now, I'm alert and symptom free for up to eight hours, when I take as directed."

Fred: "That's great, Bill." (sneeze).

Bill: "Maybe you should try Fabu-Phen, Fred. As with any new drug routine, you should first consult your physician. I'm here to tell you, side effects are mild to moderate, after the rampant diarrhea, stomach cramps and bumpy rash disappear. Some people have suffered terrible, agonizing deaths while using Fabu-Phen, but those results are not typical."

Fred: "I'll contact my family physician right away. I can't wait to improve my quality of life and golf game with Fabu-Phen."

Since the bombardment of such commercials, I have noticed my health is declining. My legs never gave me an ounce of trouble — except for the fact that they seem drawn to any nearby ice cream counter — until I realized I'm suffering from Restless Leg Syndrome. Now, whenever I see that commercial with the tiny tacks poking that poor woman's shins, my legs tingle for hours. Come to think of it, my toes always itch whenever I see that little creature crawl up under that man's toenail.

And then there's my bone health to consider. Grandmother does have osteoporosis and my back was sore the other day after that three-mile hike.

I'd better make an appointment with my doct…physician.

I think I'll also ask her if she thinks I need some of that anti-nausea stuff because I feel queasy whenever that little animated blob of mucous wearing the beer-stained T-shirt comes on the screen.

I hope that's not contraindicated but if it is, I can take some of that stuff that results in blurred vision next time that commercial comes on.

Machines don't understand Southern accents

Here's a philosophical question: Have you really cursed if the bad words are heard only by a machine?

I recently had the opportunity to test this theory.

I've noticed that, with increasing frequency, I am expected to talk to machines. I have also noticed they are either not programmed to understand the subtleties of the Southern accent, or they're programmed to drive us to therapy.

I've also noticed the recorded voices are those of women and I wonder if the company execs figure fewer people will be driven to violence by a soothing female voice.

When I recently called my credit card company, a friendly, if monotonous, mechanical voice asked me to press or say '1' if I wanted to speak in English. I was tempted to say "*uno*," but I politely said, "One."

"I'm sorry," the voice says, sounding as sincere as if it had just heard my dog died. "I didn't understand you. Please press or say '1'..."

I pushed the button.

The voice also didn't understand my next request or the next, until I said in disgust, "I want to talk to a human being! Can somebody find me a human being to talk to?"

It sounds like some modern-day version of the line from those 1950s sci-fi films: "Take me to your leader."

My next breakdown came when I called a toll-free information line.

"Please say the listing you request now," the chirpy voice requested.

"Lone Star Steakhouse," I said.

"I heard: 'Loser Fakeout,'" the voice responds. "Is that correct?"

"No," I say.

"Please repeat the listing now."

I enunciate: "Lone-*star* Steak-*house*."

"I heard: 'Porn Star Cake Joust.' Is that correct?"

I sighed into the phone.

"I heard: 'Hyundai dealership.' Is that correct?"

"I was only sighing…"

"I heard…"

Enough was enough. "Oh, hush up, wouldya and let me talk to a real live, individual!"

"I heard: 'Neil's Live Bait and Tackle.' Is that correct?"

"X#*@!"

"I heard: 'X#*@!' We are instructed not to listen to obscenities. Goodbye."

I listened to the dial tone for a second, then shrugged.

That time, it was correct.

Men swapping advice? Be afraid

Ladies, it seems men have overstepped their boundaries — again.

First it was guylights for their hair, then guyliner and manscara, then mantyhose. (About a dozen guys wrote me to say male pantyhose are worn for comfort or aiding circulation. Only one writer listed his reason for wearing pantyhose as "fetish." To which I responded, "Alrighty then.")

Now, men are trying to steal one of women's most-anticipated birthrights — the wedding shower.

Little girls spend their youth dreaming dreams of tiny cucumber sandwiches with the crusts cut off, sherbet punch and games like Bride Bingo.

And men are horning in on our action.

Apparently, though, they think they are too good for recipe swaps and bow-quets — instead, they want to play poker and drinking games while their guests bring gifts of power tools and sporting equipment wrapped with newspapers and duct tape.

They already get their own male-themed cakes at the wedding, they get to go on the honeymoon — now they've gotta get greedy?

Themanregistry.com lists gifts like flasks and bar stools and suggests taking guests on a brewery tour or golfing. The site also states: "The party doesn't have to involve any mention of your wedding day. Consider it a pre-wedding bash that serves as a great excuse to hang out with your male friends."

Isn't that called a bachelor party?

And with Lowe's Home Improvement adding a wedding registry, it seems this trend is only likely to grow.

Women, beware. It seems men are trading more than high-fives at these shindigs — they are swapping *advice*.

You read it right.

Some men are apparently telling the groom-to-be how to extricate himself from his wife's annoying presence (go into another room with the Xbox) or how to win an argument.

This, we cannot stand for.

For decades, we women have relied on the fact that men don't talk about personal things. While we were busy sharing the secrets to men's strengths and weaknesses, learning to keep them in their place, how to win every battle, men were busy sharing sports statistics and bathroom humor.

Keeping them in check has been, we have to say it, relatively simple.

With all this male bonding, the tide could turn.

Be vigilant, ladies. Don't give your man time for male bonding. If you have to buy a 60-inch HD TV to keep him home, do it.

We stand to lose everything — except maybe childbirth and brassieres.

Oh, and those little cucumber sandwiches.

Try an ice-cold Cow-ca Cola

I try not to be judgmental. Really, I do.

But when someone says he wants to make a soft drink from cow urine, I admit my first reaction is to think he was dropped on his head as a baby — from an airplane.

The idea of drinking a bovine pee cola gives a whole new meaning to those old Peter Frampton lyrics, "I'm in you, urine me." At least I think that's how they went.

Plus, it makes you give those Red Bull ingredients a second glance.

According to a report in the UK's Times Online, a Hindu nationalist group charged with protecting India's sacred cows plans to create such a drink, which could be ready to market by the end of the year.

The head of the group told The Times the drink won't smell like urine.

Whew. There's one worry off my mind. You won't have to smell the cow pee while you taste it. As we've learned from that new Pepto-Bismol flavor, a little cherry scent can cover a myriad of creepy taste sensations.

Seems members of this group were frustrated by the Westernization of India, which includes rising popularity of Coca-Cola and Pepsi.

Maybe they're right. Maybe Cow-ca Cola or Pee-psi — or even Dr. Pee-per — are just the things needed to compete.

Think of the options: Diet Cow-ca Cola, Cherry Cow-ca Cola, Cow-ca Cola Zero with no carbs. You could make Cow-ca Cola floats, Cow-ca Cola cakes — the possibilities are endless.

Plus, I'm thinking the main ingredient is probably free — and free-flowing.

These people may be on to the largest marketing coup in decades. They say they hope to some day export their drink.

Somehow, I don't think it will make the leap to North America.

Over here, we will ingest whatever preservatives that make Twinkies stay fresh after two millennia in a lunchbox and some of us will even drink soy milk but, as we did with "New Coke," which if I remember tasted like cow pee, we have to draw the line somewhere.

That Hindu guy said the new cola will prove the stature given cows in Indian culture.

That's cool. As an animal lover, I think living alongside cows actually sounds like a pretty fun idea, except maybe I wouldn't want one to sleep on the foot of my bed like my cat does. Kneading its hooves on my stomach to wake me for breakfast could get a little painful.

But here in America, we like our cows cute, like on the Chick-fil-A billboards or the California cheese commercials filled with happy, talking bovines.

So I'll wait for the commercial that shows a cow drinking a can of its own urine before I decide.

Or until they put a sticker on the label that says cow urine kills fat cells. Then I'll buy it by the caseload.

She stomped on his heart, so he wants his kidney back

For centuries, we women have gotten a bad rap — you know, the old saying about "a woman scorned" and all.

But I am here to tell you, sometimes a spurned man can react with every bit as much fury as a woman, which we all know can make your brains turn to Cream of Wheat that's set on the stove too long.

Take, for instance, the New York surgeon who announced in January that, if he couldn't have the wife he was divorcing, he'd take back his kidney — the one he donated to save her life.

Just to be clear — the kidney is *inside her body* now.

We have to assume they liked each other better at the time.

But, her cheatin' heart allegedly led her astray and her hubby, Dr. Richard Batista, wanted his due, according to an Associated Press article. Thankfully, his many years as a surgeon taught him to be realistic and, likely realizing taking back a kidney would be both bloody *and* not covered by his HMO, he decided he'd settle for $1.5 million from the soon-to-be-ex-missus.

He claimed he was doing it for the good of the children.

Some child psychologist somewhere just went *"ka-ching."*

Couldn't the good doctor just do what all great country music artists do and write a song about his achy breaky heart?

Something along the lines of: "I'll Never Feel Whole While My Kidney's in You," or "My Piano's Broke so I Want My Organ Back?"

That should make him feel all better.

In the meantime, maybe he should change his organ donor card to say "organ loaner."

I'm going out on a limb here, but I think there should be a rule that once you've filtered a few glasses of Cold Duck through a kidney, it should be yours to keep.

It's not like the scroll saw you loaned to the neighbor, for criminy's sake.

But Dr. Batista is not the only scorned man who wanted his ex's body — literally.

Another AP article stated that Thomas Lee Rowley was on trial last month in California for allegedly stabbing his ex-girlfriend six times in an effort to get back the breast implants he bought her.

How could she have let go of such a romantic? Most women only get chocolates for Valentine's Day but she got some serious bon bons, know what I'm sayin'?

Alas, she left him and he, according to police, was determined to get what was rightfully his, even if it was, well, inside her body.

The woman survived the attack to testify against him. Her breasts weren't so lucky. Apparently, those things, like waterbeds, have an aversion to sharp points.

The good news is, the implants have been re-inflated.

Maybe she should send the bill to Rowley.

After all, a trip to a good "body" shop ain't cheap.

I think I'll put that to music.

Does Octo-Mom have oatmeal for brains?

That mom who just had eight babies better hope at least one can play the drums and they all look cute in color-coordinated, bell-bottomed jumpsuits.

They're going to need some means of support and, since Nadya Suleman already has six kids, no job and no house, it seems putting a kid band on the road à la Partridge Family or Brady Bunch may be their best hope.

I know people are questioning how responsible this woman can be to purposely put herself, 14 children and us taxpayers in this situation — but, me?

I just have one, OK three, questions for her:

Did the pilot light between your ears go out?

Was your brain recalled?

Did you get the drugs *before* conception?!

I mean, I'm glad we don't live in China where reproduction is regulated and I agree everyone has the right to make her own choices but she obviously gave no thought to how these babies would get raised. Trust me, it will take a village — the size of Australia.

This isn't a litter of puppies. They won't be content with a bowl of water on the floor, a sofa to chew and an antique rug to pee on.

She'd need at least eight arms at feeding time and she didn't have but two last time I looked, despite her lovely media nickname, Octo Mom, which sounds like Spider-Man's latest archenemy.

I hold Headline News host Nancy Grace and her wannabe Jane Velez Mitchell personally responsible for these ridiculous nicknames: Tot Mom for Casey Anthony, Octo Mom for Suleman. Next, they'll be calling the woman who bathed and drank wine with that killer chimp Monkey Mom, although I admit that one kind of has a nice ring to it.

But back to Octo.

No one's asked Mom yet how she managed to carry eight babies with a back injury that left her on disability.

She couldn't even think of enough names so all eight babies have the same middle name: Noah Angel, Maliah Angel, Isaiah Angel, Nariah Angel, Makai Angel, Josiah Angel, Jeremiah Angel and Jonah Angel.

Has she thought beyond diapers?

Probably not, since the thought of 560 Pampers a week is enough to melt your brain (and olfactory nerves).

So here's some food for thought:

- Eight ball teams
- Eight teachers annually
- Eight class plays annually
- 2,998 teacher conferences
- 4,960 sick days
- Eight proms
- Eight prom *dates*
- Eight cars
- Eight insurance policies

According to babycenter.com, it will cost $1.5 million to raise these babies to age 18, if none of them have permanent disabilities. Mom probably shouldn't think beyond age 18: eight colleges, eight weddings, eight sons- and daughters-in-law. No one's brain deserves that kind of abuse, even a brain that appears to be filled with dreams of fame, or oatmeal. Either seems equally likely.

I'm just sayin.'

A feel-good column
for uncertain economic times

I know I don't typically write about mushy, feel-good stuff but in these tough economic times, I had the urge to spread some optimism.

In today's column, you will read about heroes, people who refuse to give up hope, no matter what challenges they face.

It is my dream you will find yourselves feeling renewed after hearing these inspiring tales.

Let's start with Sheyla Hershey, a 28-year-old Houston woman. The determined wife and mother has undergone 11 surgeries and knows there are more in her future. But she won't give up. Why?

Sheyla's goal is to have the world's biggest, er, chest.

After all those surgeries, she is now a 38KKK and is looking to go up a letter, which if her bra strap breaks, a likely enough scenario, will give new meaning to the phrase "all L breaking loose."

So far, unbelievably, the Guinness Book of World Records has bypassed Sheyla in favor of someone named Maxi Mounds. But leave it to Sheyla to turn sour grapes into grapefruits. When asked why she continues to try for such an inflated goal, Sheyla replied, "I had a dream."

Makes you misty, doesn't it?

Next on our list of optimists is a 68-year-old South Korean woman who won't let anything keep her from her dream of one day driving a car. Except for the little matter of a driver's license, she is ready to take the wheel. All she needs to do is pass the test – on her 772nd try later this year.

I admire her pluck but if she finally succeeds, I plan to steer clear, so to speak, of the entire country of South Korea.

Another woman who is filled with hope is Linda Wolfe of Anderson, Ind. After being married 23 times — most of her former husbands died but some were divorced, according to news reports — Linda is once again looking for love.

Here is a woman who obviously believes in the sanctity and commitment of marriage, so much so she holds the Guinness Book of World Records for most married person.

She's had three times as many marriages as Elizabeth Taylor, eight times more than Donald Trump and 23 times more than Miley Cyrus.

A woman who's willing to take on a 24th husband is filled with more stupidity, er, optimism than I knew existed.

You go, girl.

Last but not least are some true entrepreneurs. Keeping a business afloat these days may be difficult but the company Wallypop has a unique product, one that's sure to be a keeper.

Visit living/wallypop.net/wipes to order your very own set of cloth toilet wipes.

I know what you're thinking: Do what? Say who?

They are just what they sound like — toilet wipes that you do not throw away. Instead you wash and dry them to use again.

Hey, you want to save the environment, don't you?

In a How to Use section of the site, which I thought rather presumptuous, the makers state using Wallypop wipes is "not nearly as gross as you might think."

Uh-huh.

It continues: "… there is a certain ick factor."

Ya think?

And then it discusses how to set the wipes in a decorative basket on the back of the toilet once they've been cleaned. "Our wipes have minimal stain," it says.

I'm here to tell you I don't want to visit a house with used wipes on the back of the toilet, even those with "minimal stain." Especially those with "minimal stain."

I don't even want to look at my own stains, thank you.

But you have to give them credit for trying to leave their, er, mark in the business world.

Well, that's it for today.

I hope you have that warm feeling in your heart.

After all, I had a dream.

Quick! Put out an Amber Bock Alert!

OK, class, last week we learned about people who remain optimistic in the face of tough challenges.

You know: When the going gets psychotic, the psychotic get going. That type thing.

This week, we'll learn about those who handle dire straits a little differently, or, as I like to put it: "Seriously whacked out times call for seriously whacked out measures."

To some, the people described below are heroes, people who won't let anything — not crooks, not oncoming cars, not the sense God gave a thumbtack — stand in their way.

To others, these people are just, well, a few peanuts shy of a recall.

Take the grocery store clerk in Fullerton, Calif., who noticed a man who was trying to make off with a 36-pack of beer. The brave clerk was not one to let innocent brew get beernapped. Who knew if this thief would properly care for the beer? Who knew when the grocery would ever see it again?

It seemed like the perfect time for an Amber Bock Alert.

Instead, the clerk raced after the man and did what any responsible beer lover would do — jumped on the hood of the getaway car and hung on for four blocks despite the fact that the thief kept speeding up and then hitting his brakes in an attempt to knock the man off. Finally, the tired thief stopped the car.

The clerk then retrieved the beer but left the thief, who drove off, for police to find.

Like I always say, "A beer in the hand is worth two in the crook." Or something like that.

Next we have a Florida woman, who last week saw an injustice and did what we've all been taught to do — called the police.

The problem was, McDonald's was out of Chicken McNuggets. Look, y'all, don't judge. I know those things are more cardboard than chicken and sometimes there are mysterious little gray bits inside them.

But this woman wanted some and, in fact, had already paid. When she was told the restaurant was out of McNuggets, she did what any sane-minded woman would do and asked for her money back. The clerk said that particular McDonald's had a no-refund policy and the customer would just have to accept a Big Mac or McRib or something.

Say what?

The woman didn't want any McRib.

She wanted her McNUGGETS, people!

I happen to back her on this. In this economy, we should get what we pay for, right? Even gray-ish, chicken-like, disc-shaped food products.

So she picked up her cell phone and dialed 911. Not once, not twice, but three times.

Seems police don't think absence of McNuggets is an emergency. (But let Dunkin Donuts run dry, and, well…)

McDonald's has since apologized and refunded the money but the woman may be McScarred for life.

Elsewhere in Florida, on Wednesday, a man trying to save a parking space for his wife at a Murphy USA gas station stood in the space waiting for her to pull up.

Another driver pulled into the spot and intentionally struck the man in the knees. Then he backed up and did it again, witnesses said.

Well, sure. I can see that. Apparently, no one told the "victim" about the "no holdies" rule. Who wouldn't be upset at this break in parking lot etiquette?

The victim's knees were bruised and swollen, according to The News-Press in Fort Myers. He will survive and likely emerge a better citizen.

See? People are coming together.

As a nation, we are saying, "Lean on me … and I will push your fat hindend right off."

It warms my heart.

Section 3

This #*&! from New York City!?!
Small-town America knows doodie when it calls

Are New Yorkers
beyond the call of 'doodie?'

Whew!

What a relief. Crisis averted.

I could smell a fight brewing when some Limestone County residents recently raised a stink and some strategically worded signs about a local "doodie farm," where human waste was being spread on crops as fertilizer.

Not only is this "humanure" unsafe, opponents say, it smells to high heaven.

Well.

I'm not sure how that fragrance thing got by farmers before they decided to use the stuff (Maybe they thought *eau de toilet* meant…nah.)

Is it any wonder their neighbors are flush with anger?

In case you missed it, here's the poop: Officials at Synagro Technologies have agreed not to use any more processed sewer sludge on local pastures after Limestone County Commissioners sought an injunction, saying they're not taking any crap. The company will continue to use "the product" on "remote" areas after it is worked into the soil rather than spread on top in an effort to reduce the smell. Better still, the processing company will seek to make the sewer sludge smell more pleasant in the future.

Good luck with that. They better get Martha Stewart on that project, pronto.

What seemed to bother people more, though, than the fact that someone past the age of 2 doesn't know better than to spread doodie around, was the news that this particular, er, stuff, came from New York City.

It was like someone dropped a bomb.

You could almost hear the collective voice of the county raised in the high-pitched, disbelieving cry of the Pace salsa slogan, "This *#%@'s from *New York City*?!"

I could understand it.

It's offensive that those arrogant New Yorkers decided that what goes through their toilets belongs on Alabamians' future food.

And if we were disposed to spread sewer sludge on crops, couldn't we find some local poop? Or at the very least, regional?

I can't imagine there's a shortage. It's one natural resource that keeps going, and going, and going...

Could be, with all those alligators living in New York City sewers, they ran out of space to store theirs.

I'm guessing most of you, like me, didn't know there was such a thing as human waste fertilizer. And most of you, like me, could have lived, say, another 80 years without the knowledge.

But we have been forced to become experts in excrement.

We learned that although chemically treated sewer sludge was approved by the Environmental Protection Agency for this use, some people are concerned it contains dangerous bacteria and could make our families sick.

Let's review.

It has a smell no striking of a match can dissipate, it contains bacteria, it is typically found in diapers and toilets (though sometimes on walls if you have a toddler), and someone has to pay to process it before it can be spread.

And that's an improvement on good, old-fashioned cow patties....how?

It's not like there's a higher, Nobel-winning purpose here, like the creation of human waste "bio-gas" to provide power in Rwandan prisons. Problem: too many prisoners, nowhere to put the waste, expensive power. Solution: Poo-power.

Now inmates eat food cooked on stoves that run on the methane-type fuel.

While I would hesitate to eat a gas-powered steak, this, at least, is an admirable use.

I tried to find the good in our local situation. Really, I did.

The lesson, it seems to me, is simple: Fences make good neighbors. Feces? Not so much.

Seed-spittin' is an American right

Y'all, I'm taking a produce stand.

I can no longer sit back and watch the de-seeding of America.

We must save the last great American pastime — watermelon seed spitting.

When aiming a seed at the bridge of your brother's nose (just so you can be fascinated by how it makes his eyes cross when one lands there), you never heard your mother say, "Stop that before you put someone's eye out."

You don't need to buckle up or wear a helmet (although you never know where one of those little suckers might land. Earmuffs may be advisable).

I don't think anyone's ever been maimed by a watermelon seed, unless you count the trauma of wondering if your dad was joking when he said a vine would grow in your stomach from that seed you swallowed.

And how many things can you use as a weapon on your brother that, if you happen to miss, will land and grow into one of nature's most perfect foods?

Now mad scientists are trying to take that away from us.

If you've been in a grocery store lately, you'll notice pile after pile of small, round, pale, pitiful melons.

Gone are the oblong, green-striped beauties of my childhood. Gone is the thrill of searching for the largest one and having your dad hoist it on his shoulder to take home.

Gone are the seeds.

I am planning a boycott. Call me if you want to join SOWS (Save our Watermelon Seeds) and help paint signs with slogans like "Spittin' is an American right," or "A seed for every American!"

Jack Dietz can be our spokesman. Don't tell me you don't recognize the name — he holds the world record for spitting a seed the farthest: 66 feet, 11 inches.

He's a role model for my daughter.

Just last summer, while aiming for the lens of my glasses, Shannon landed a seed or 20 right between the Gerbera daisies and snapdragons in the bed next to the driveway.

Two weeks later, I had to park my car on the street to keep from running over the vine.

She grew eight fruits and it was one of my proudest moments as a mother to watch her take a bite of a watermelon she grew herself.

It's what we parents dream of, that our kids can experience the same pleasures we had as children, feeling the summer air go cool on arms and legs sticky with watermelon juice, watching your mom gather the rinds to cut for pickles, and having your dad hose you off in the yard after yelling, "You kids better not step foot in the house like that."

Those were the days.

The next generation could grow up seedless. Forced to take up more dangerous and violent activities, they'll soon become statistics of their forefathers' short-sightedness.

Write your congressperson and beg for non-genetically mutated melons.

Tell the governor to stop the madness.

We have the power, people.

We can't let them rob Americans of the tradition and romance that is seed spitting.

Take action now and plant the seeds of hope for the future.

Who can blame Nanny for hoofing it?

It's got to be an unimaginable life: Sold like chattel, left homeless, chased by police and nearly Tasered.

Now, Nanny is an escape goat.

It has to be said, so I'm saying it: "Leave her alone! After all she's been through! Leave Nanny alone!"

A stray nanny goat's on the lam in Decatur, Ala. — which is against the law because she's classified as livestock — after police were unable to Taser her into submission last week.

Can anyone blame Nanny for hoofing it? This is the land of goat stews, for pity's sake. No church, volunteer fire department or school in a three-county radius can hold a fundraiser without selling goat stew by the bowl, quart or gallon. Boss Hill, top purveyor of goat stew in Elkmont, was quoted in an area newspaper describing the best method to catch Nanny the goat.

If that doesn't turn a goat chicken, I don't know what will.

Please, I'm beggin' ya, give Nanny a break.

For weeks, she's lived by her wits, seeking shelter beneath an old shed, residents say. She crossed a busy street, looking both ways, to nibble cemetery grass. Who's she bothering, really? Saves gas in the mower.

Now she wanders alone, likely too humiliated by the sale tag stapled into her hide to return to her family.

For two weeks, she's eluded capture by authorities and watchful residents reporting sightings.

They may be intent on getting their goat, but I say they're taking it too far.

What's next?

A call to Dog the Bounty Hunter?

A song entitled, "Run, Nanny, Run?"

A Lifetime movie about her capture: "Goatbusters?"

I'm glad America's Most Wanted is no longer on the air.

Can't you let her live in peace?

At the very least, use the Barney Fife method: Have someone lure Nanny with soothing harmonica music to a lush, green field where she can live out her days frolicking, looking for love with Billy and maybe having a few kids.

Years from now, she'd be only a memory and an episode on "Cold Case."

If you can't find a harmonica player, give me a call. I've got a backyard that needs mowing and I like feta cheese.

She'd be safe with me. I don't even know how to cook.

So you think Southerners sound un-eje-macayted?

Y'all, I'm fixin' to have a come-apart. I'd heard about yokels who teach people how to speak without a Southern accent, but I didn't know it was becoming downright trendy to want to "talk right," i.e., like you ain't from these parts.

Don't that jar your preserves?

A true Southern accent, as all of us know, is a thing of beauty, like a honeysuckle-scented breeze against your ear. But to some— i.e., the nuts in Hollywood—it is a country-sounding twang or an exaggerated whine that grates on your nerves like the sound of a leaf blower's motor outside your bedroom window at 2 a.m.

Note to movie-types: Scarlett and Rhett are not real.

Neither are their accents.

We Southerners have known it for years — it's about time you did.

I know; it's a shocker.

And while you're already off balance, I'll go ahead and give you the rest: We don't live on plantations, or ask the name of your great-grandaddy's grandaddy, and, with the exception of a few re-enacters, none of us refer to it as "the War of Northern Aggression."

I have never sat on a chay-uh or drunk wah-tuh.

I don't know the words to "Dixie."

Not the tiniest sip of a mint julep has ever passed my lips, and, take a deep breath, some of us have been to college.

I myself am the recipient of hi-yah eje-macayshun.

The desire for that educated polish, it seems, is the reason these "How to Lose Your Southern Accent" courses are cropping up. Several professors of

103

such courses stated that Southern accents make people seem less educated and refined. It's difficult to be taken seriously or get a job if you speak "Southern," they say.

Well, butter me and call me a biscuit.

Many course descriptions also state they teach actors how to lose their accents so they can get more jobs.

Mebbe they should oughta spend their time teaching correct Southern accents so we don't have to cringe when we watch "Steel Magnolias," "Forrest Gump," or any movie made from a John Grisham novel.

That is why Lucas Black is my hero. Lucas, who is from a small Alabama town, is a young actor who has had much success without changing his accent. It was his very real northern Alabama accent that got him his first film part (in Kevin Costner's "The War") and he's managed to find plenty of roles since, including the young boy in Billy Bob Thornton's acclaimed "Sling Blade." More recently, he starred in "Friday Night Lights," and "The Fast and the Furious 3: Tokyo Drift."

So far, he hasn't sold out. He turned down a part in "The Horse Whisperer" because the producers wanted him to learn to speak without his accent.

Black has said he doesn't want to change who he is.

He must not have seen, or cared about, the results of a 1999 study by Michigan State University professor Dennis Preston, in which 150 Michigan residents were asked to rank the "correctness" of English spoken in all 50 states. The South ranked the lowest, with Alabama at the bottom of the list.

Hmmm. Reckon if we polled 150 Alabamians, they might think people from Dee-troyt talk funny?

One professor of such a course said some Southern accents are so strong an interpreter is needed to translate. Yet he could understand Nicholas Cage in "Con Air?"

Yet another professor and linguistic expert, Patricia Cukor-Avila with the University of North Texas, said people outside the South associate the Southern accent with laziness, ignorance and backward thinking, which has given us "linguistic insecurity."

Do what?

Say who?

If only I'd known. I could have started a fund, or at least a support group for Southerners Insecure about Linguistics and Language Y'all (or SILLY).

Well, I'm getting myself shut of all this rigamarole. It makes me no nevermind if some snooty people think I don't talk right.

They cain't hep it if'n their mamas didn't raise them right.

Bless their hearts.

Finally, the reason chickens cross the road

The scanner crackled in the newsroom Monday and we were able to make out the words, "chickens," and "in the middle of the road."

Like all good reporters, we went immediately on alert.

Dead chickens?

Live ones?

Chickens stranded mid-crossing?

We didn't know.

Then we heard an officer give the location of the alleged fowl play, a road near the local poultry plant.

That's when we realized: Some death-row chickens had made a run for it.

Charges of attempting to elude police could be forthcoming. This kind of excitement is what we live for.

I picked up the phone and called our photographer, who was out on assignment.

"Kim," I said, "I need you to get to Hobbs Street and shoot some chickens in the road."

Sending paparazzi to take advantage of what could very well be the chickens' last, desperate moments could seem heartless (What if a despondent chicken attempted to leap to his death down a drainage ditch? What if a crazed hen shaved her head in a bid for attention?), but this is the news business and an incident of chickens crossing the road is no joking matter.

Kim, whose name I promised to mention here after she complained I sent her on a "wild chicken chase," called me twice from her cell phone.

"I don't see any chickens," she said finally. "Are you sure you heard right?" She called the police department and got the coop, er, scoop: A single chicken had managed to escape the confines of a poultry truck and hit the road.

Like poultry in motion, the chicken fled and, though we were without an award-winning photo for the front page, we inwardly cheered the chicken's bravado and wished him Godspeed.

Then we went home and had chicken cacciatore for dinner.

Hypocritical? Sure.

But people can't help but root for the underchicken.

In Los Angeles — whose police department, unlike the one in Athens, Ala., probably does not have a radio code for livestock that means "Quick! Send a patrol car! Cows are blocking the road to the Goodtime Jamboree" — residents continue to champion a brood of chickens that took up residence four decades ago along the Hollywood Freeway.

I'm not making this up. I would kid about a lot of things, but not about homeless poultry.

At one time, there was even a video game based on the "Freeway Chickens," as the colony is known.

According to lore, the chickens were liberated from a poultry farmer during an unfortunate trucking accident and staked out turf under the Vineland Avenue ramp.

Soon the chickens, apparently realizing there was safety in numbers and also that Californians consider eating meat a sin worse than voting Republican, numbered in the thousands.

Years later, city leaders wrangled as many chickens as they could and took them to a farm (at least, that's the story they told the newspapers, although there reportedly was an abundance of new chicken dishes at area restaurants that week), but the few uncatchable chickens did as chickens are wont to do and multiplied. The chickens are still there today, fat and sassy from the scraps of tofu and bean curd thrown by California motorists.

Soon I was to learn that Athens has the beginnings of its own Chicken Underground.

A local woman, who remains nameless lest she be harassed by authorities or held up to the ridicule that befalls most forward-thinkers, rescues chickens that leap, fall or are pushed by their sacrificing mothers onto the roadside as poultry trucks pass her neighborhood.

Currently, she is caring for two liberated chickens, welcoming them as part of her family.

I like to think these pet chickens cluck urgently as poultry trucks roll past the house, spreading the word to others so that they, too, can taste freedom.

Maybe this liberator managed to hide Monday's fugitive fowl. Maybe he made it, at long last, to the other side of the road.

I like to think so. Otherwise, I wouldn't be able to look at a bucket of extra-crispy wings without shedding a tear.

And that might ruin the taste.

Celebrating Getting Yakked on At Work Day

Some guy in Seattle woke up one recent morning and thought to himself, "Hmmm. I think I'll take Toshi to work with me today," which may not seem such an odd thought until you learn that Toshi is a yak — and I don't mean he's talkative.

Jim Harding, CEO of a small software company called Cirqe, decided bringing one of the critters from his yak ranch — who knew? — to the office would shake things up and inspire creativity.

So, shovel in hand — seems yaks aren't litter trained — he brought the half-ton, long-haired, horned beast to work last week.

The yak, and thus Jim, got a lot of publicity, but personally, I don't see how this could be that different from Take Your Kids to Work Day.

Unruly hair in eyes? Check.

Gold ring in nose? Check.

Mysterious substance deposited on conference room floor? Check, ewww, and check.

And on Take Your Kids to Work Day, someone is sure to leave a half-eaten, lint-covered lollipop in the boss' desk drawer, use Photoshop to black out teeth and add a hairy nose wart to the publisher's image in the company photo, and have a newsroom shoot-out armed with a couple of staplers.

And that's just the grown-ups.

No, really, it's probably not a bad idea to shake things up, change the typical work-a-day attitude by doing something different.

That's why I plan to bring my cat Butthea...er, Scout, to work next week.

He may weigh 10 pounds instead of 1,000 and he doesn't have horns, but he does yak a lot — especially when I've just cleaned my carpet.

Besides, Scout was plenty hissed off when he heard some nuts, er, dog lovers came up with National Take Your Dog to Work Day. There is no such day of honor for our much cleaner and better-behaved feline friends. If that's not prejudice, I don't know what is. I'm thinking of suing on Scout's behalf and trust me, I *will* play the species card. Maybe I can get Toshi to join us and we'll file a class action suit.

If I brought Scout to work, I think he could bring a lot to the table, specifically, furballs.

In our conference room, by which I mean a small area of carpet partitioned on one side by a half wall, we hold a weekly budget meeting to discuss which stories we will write for the newspaper in the coming week, by which I mean we sit around and say, "I hope someone robs someone Thursday. Looks like a slow news day."

Scout, when he was finished shredding and eating his copy of the story budget, could give some input.

"Puuu-u-rr-rr," he might say, meaning, "Where's the food?"

And then "Mrr-ow hisss," meaning, *"Where's the food?"*

Then perhaps "Yo-o-ow," meaning "Does it *look* like I'm joking?"

He might then decide, as he often does at home, that leaping from the head of one person to another is a suitable means of getting from Point A to Point Wherever the Food is Stored.

This would result in more yowls and hisses, this time from the owners of said heads because, of course, Scout would need to use his claws to gain proper leverage for leaping, the motion of which would likely lead to his yakking in someone's hair.

So while people may leave the weekly meeting scratched, bloodied and yakked upon, I feel sure the incident would inspire creativity.

After all, there is no end to the names you can call a butthea…er, cat.

There's a little redneck woman in all of us

I have never been so proud of my roots, and I don't mean the dark stripe on top of my head.

Today, I can stand tall and announce I grew up in Warner Robins, Ga., home of championship football and Little League teams, a top-notch Air Force base, and a couple who recently celebrated their nuptials by jumping into a mud pit.

Hey, I'm not judging.

I myself am no stranger to mud pits. We have our very own annual Mud Volleyball Tournament right here in Athens, Ala., and I once was a member of the Dirty Dozen.

I am also no stranger to unusual — some might say *redneck* — wedding rituals. I once threw instant grits at my uncle and his bride when his wedding was held at our home.

Well. We were out of rice.

But I can't top the wedding of Rawni and Rob "Robo" Sprague, who were married July 5 at the annual Redneck Summer Games in Dublin, Ga.

Reporter Ashley Tusan Joyner writes in the Macon Telegraph that the reunited childhood sweethearts went all out on a fancy wedding, which was filmed for an upcoming episode of CMT's "My Big Fat Redneck Wedding."

Rawni and Robo, which I assume is pronounced "Robbo" and not "Robo" as in RoboCop, became engaged during a race at the Talladega Motor Speedway in October.

That auspicious beginning led Rawni to carefully plan a ceremony that is sure to become the stuff of legend among her children and grandchildren. No detail was left undone:

Confederate flag bikini top under gown? $10.99.

Confederate flag garter belt? $3.99 with coupon.

Confederate flag-decorated acrylic nails? $4.99 plus custom painting.

Bottle-cap earrings? Cost of two beers.

Jack Daniels bottle to hold the bouquet? Priceless.

I'm glad I wasn't there to see the couple's first dance to "Hold My Beer." I don't think I could have held back the tears.

The article doesn't say if the couple jumped in the mud before or after the first dance, but in my mind, I like to picture Robo lovingly wiping mud from Rawni's belly-button ring during the dance.

"He was always the one," Rawni is quoted in the story.

Awww.

Now I'm really gonna cry.

Really, I have Jeff Foxworthy to thank for my moment of pride.

It was Jeff who made redneck cool, who made porch sofas and year-round Christmas lights fashionable.

It was Jeff whose creative genius gave the world "You might be a redneck" Christmas balls, the Redneck Dictionary, and the pregnant bride figurine.

Without him, would the people of Dublin have felt secure enough to throw a party featuring Bobbin' for Pigs Feet, Armpit Serenades and a Miss Redneck competition?

Would Rawni's bridesmaids have felt free to wear their Daisy Dukes and gingham crop tops?

No. They would have been shamed into taffeta horrors the color of orange sherbet, spreading suffering throughout the land.

So, Jeff, I raise my bottle to you.

After that, I'll raise another one.

What good is one bottle-cap earring?

Boy bands have changed since we basked in glow of Donny's teeth

In the newsroom one day, we started talking about childhood pop star crushes.

Mine was Donny Osmond, who made girls melt when he sang "Puppy Love."

Oh, how I wanted to grow up to be Mrs. Donny Osmond.

But then love's bloom faded, which is probably for the best because in recent years I've begun to suspect the Osmonds are responsible for global warming.

The glow given off by their collective teeth had to have some impact on the ozone layer for all those years. I don't see how Al Gore could have overlooked this theory, except that he never smiles and therefore it didn't occur to him his book should have been called "An Inconvenient Tooth."

But when I was 10, nothing was as exciting as a teenage boy in a tight, mini-Elvis jumpsuit, dripping fringe, sweat and charisma. I would watch my television and bask in the glow of Donny's grin, dreaming one day I could polish each and every tooth…

Oh…OK, I'm back.

The change in boy bands since then is disturbing. Can you imagine Justin Timberlake wearing a fringed jumpsuit and singing, "You're too sweet and innocent for me" instead of grinding his hips and bringing SexyBack?

Our photographer Kim Rynders was in love with Leif Garrett, but I didn't like him because his Farrah-Fawcett feathers were prettier than mine and his satin jeans were tighter. No one felt more vindicated when he grew up bald and skanky looking.

'Do rags are not a good look for men over 40 who spent many years doing drugs and their faces look like it.

What? I'm just sayin.'

We 40-somethings in the newsroom then debated the pros and cons of Shaun vs. David Cassidy and reporter Jean Cole threw in a vote for Bobby Sherman, but he was always singing about some girl named Julie, which was a deal-breaker for me.

Jennifer Hill, who, it should be noted, is at least 14 years younger than the rest of us, had the hots for New Kids on the Block. I guess that name was all well and good when the group's members were teenagers but, really, didn't anyone plan beyond those first few years of fame?

I guess Skanky Old Dudes on the Assisted Living Floor didn't have the same ring to it.

Kidding!

Donnie Wahlberg and gang are still pretty cute, in a dad sort-of-way. They even still dance in unison, complete with synchronized spins, as evidenced by the video for their new album: "Skanky Old Dudes Perform Songs to Rinse Your Dentures By."

Kidding again.

But someone should have warned them that Boy Band World has changed and NKOTB may need hipness replacement.

These days, they can't compete with the likes of teen heartthrobs the Jonas Brothers, who have an abundance of charm and eyebrows.

Plus, they are backed by the Disney Machine, which everyone knows is the only entity on earth that might possibly have more power than Oprah.

Maybe the brothers can use their millions for a good cause.

Me? I'd invest in a personal brow waxer.

Snooty non-foodies have no business in a newsroom

We have this guy in the newsroom —I'll call him Edd Davis…mainly because that's his name — who is having a little trouble fitting in.

Oh, he's smart enough. He catches all our errors and saves us daily from complete public humiliation (who, really, wants to be responsible for the mayor making a *"pubic"* announcement or running an employment ad that says "Now hiring all shifts" without the 'F'?)

No, the work is not Edd's problem.

The problem is he doesn't understand the mission statement of newsrooms everywhere: "We eat therefore we are."

Back in the day, before my time of course, editors kept bottles of amber-colored liquids and shot glasses in their drawers and a haze of smoke hung over the desks where reporters busily puffed and typed.

In this business, we need our vices. Otherwise how would we handle people calling up and telling us how stupid we are?

But suddenly, shot glasses and cigarettes became politically incorrect, at least in public. Naturally we turned to…food.

Food of any kind, at any time, in any place.

We would even eat fruitcake. Sure, we may have to drizzle it with chocolate, but we'd eat it.

Three-day-old donuts? A minute in the microwave takes away those hard edges.

Cheese with a little greenish tinge? You don't even notice the color when it's between the bread.

And when we're not eating, we're thinking about eating.

We come in, do a couple hours of work, maybe while discussing what we had for breakfast.

Then, 'long about 10:30, we start discussing lunch options.

Chinese? Deli? Fast food?

We talk about it for about 20 minutes, then go pick it up and bring it back to our conference room, by which I mean a table surrounded by three portable walls.

At lunch we discuss important things — openings of new restaurants, recipes, the new brand of pasta we found at the store.

About an hour after lunch, spent discussing how we ate too much and now feel too sick to work, we begin discussing the afternoon snack.

Here is the most firm rule: Snacks *must include chocolate*. Always.

Shakes, cookies, pies. It doesn't matter as long as there's chocolate in there somewhere.

Several months ago, when Edd joined our merry band, we couldn't help but fall in love with the way he brought us pound cakes and Rice Krispie treats and cookies.

But then one day we wondered: Why isn't he eating these goodies himself? What kind of journalist worth his weight in Boston cream pie would share his largesse?

Finally one day he let his secret slip: "I eat to live, I don't live to eat," he said with a straight face and somewhat superior tone.

Do what?

I began to worry. I'd become accustomed to Edd's copy editing skills and his chocolate bundt cake. But surely he couldn't last in a newsroom with a sick, sad attitude like that.

Then one day, something happened that made me aware Edd wasn't a bad guy. He was just, well, a different kind of thinker.

Several of us were working late and I was bemoaning the fact that my snack drawer was devoid of chocolate. I had scraped the last Hershey kiss from the paper clip tray only hours earlier.

I was about to pledge my life for an M&M, when Edd said, "I have some of those little Snickers if you want one."

Happy happy. Joy joy.

"They're small," Edd continued. "They're not even the mini ones. They're bite sized."

I knew the difference — with a mini you might get two bites, maybe three if you were a young, inexperienced reporter. But bite-sized meant *bite*, singular. That meant you had to have at least six to equal a snack.

Still, I salivated. I managed not to jump out of my chair as Edd approached, three shining, golden-wrapped candies gleaming beneath the fluorescent lights.

Then he carefully, gently placed one on my desk.

ONE.

Was he some kind of masochist?

Did he really think a professional journalist would eat only one bite-sized Snickers bar?

That's when I understood Edd needs our sympathy, not our scorn.

We'll just keep trying to convert him, is all.

Tomorrow, we're putting a photo of an ice cream sundae as his computer wallpaper.

If you see him, help us out and slip him a Butterfinger. Bless his heart.

Know what you want before going on man hunt

Y'all will never guess — we in the South have several towns ranked among "America's Manliest Cities."

That's right — Nashville is No. 1, Charlotte is No. 2, Memphis is No. 11 and good ol' Birmingham is No. 23.

Well, don't that crank your camouflage pick-'em-up truck?

But, ladies, before you go organizing a Manly Man Hunt to any of these cities — you know, tour buses filled with rope-and-duct-tape-wielding eligible women in full-on, trap-and-keep mode — you might want to know what being "manly" means.

The survey was conducted by Combos snacks, and included such criteria as "most sports bars" and "most monster truck pulls per capita."

Huh.

So it's really a "Cities with Most Redneck Men" survey, or maybe "Cities Filled with Men Who Intend to Stay Single — For a Long, Long Time."

A report from the Manliest Cities survey states that Nashville achieved its high ranking because of its large number of NASCAR enthusiasts, the popularity of hunting and fishing and a heavy concentration of barbecue restaurants.

But let's think about this.

What right-thinking woman would choose to look for a man, say, in a city with the highest number of bowling alleys or with most power tools per capita?

Do you want a man who will help you put out the azaleas come spring, or do you want a man who's down at the Split Happens lanes rolling a few frames and sucking down a Pabst Blue Ribbon?

New Orleans also does the South proud in the Manliest Cities survey: The Big Easy boasts more hardware stores per capita than any other city in the country.

We all know the only power tools a woman wants her man to be familiar with are the vacuum and the George Foreman Grill.

Sure, it would be nice if your man were experienced with pistol-grip drills, nail guns and reciprocating saws (like anyone even knows what one of those things does) — if he would use them as God intended and you demanded. But when's the last time you saw a man use a tool from his extensive collection to actually fix something around the house that needed repairing?

Does he rehang the shutters? Fix the leaky faucet? Put a new leg on the three-legged chair in the living room that makes you have to cock your head to watch TV?

No, he uses his fancy tools on "projects," such as installing a flat-screen across from the toilet, or a handy dandy built-in keg cooler in his Barca Lounger so he can show off to other Men Who Measure Their Worth by Their Tools.

New York City, while it does have a high number of bowling alleys, is last on the Top 50 list because there's not much place there for fishing, home improvement and drag racing. Well, duh. A man who requires a bi-weekly mani-pedi and carries a Man Purse uses the word "drag" in only one context, and it has nothing to do with racing.

Did anyone really think a city where a performance of "Guys and Dolls" is a major tourist attraction and there's an art gallery on every corner would have lots of gun-toting motorheads in it?

When a New York man refers to his trigger finger, he means the one that points to the half-caf, blended cream, mochaccino at the corner Starbucks.

So now you might think I'm being picky: I don't want a man who hauls a bloody deer head into the Hair of the Dog Neighborhood Bar and Taxidermist, but I also want to be the one who carries the purse in the family.

Well, yeah.

I'm all about happy mediums.

I say a guy should never be too manly to plug in the vacuum or whip up a dinner quiche; I just don't want my guy sitting beside me at the salon with foils in his hair.

You might get past the bloody deer head, but a man discussing his guylights with a stylist is an image you can never truly erase.

Walking + texting sometimes = raw sewage

What kind of government puts warning labels on harmless-looking strollers (Do Not Fold With Infant Inside) and hair dryers (Do Not Operate While Showering) but refuses to protect its children by placing warnings on the latest and biggest threat to security of all — cell phones?

I'm not talking about the dangers of driving while talking or texting, which some governments already have taken it upon themselves to regulate. People, I'm talking about the true danger of cell phone use that the British government discovered two years ago — probably because their secret agents wear tuxes and ours don't — the threat of texting and walking at the same time.

Yes, those gray-wigged Parliamentarians in London may look ridiculous and more than slightly out of touch with reality but apparently all that powder really helps them think: they saw their citizenry walking into lampposts while texting and knocking themselves wonky, but did they laugh?

Well, probably.

But when they stopped snorting, they did the responsible thing. They went out and covered all the city's lampposts in nice, cushy foam so as to save their citizens' brains from any more bruising.

Kind of makes you go weepy, doesn't it?

Here in America, what do our governments do?

In Staten Island, N.Y., the sewer department leaves off manhole covers so teenage girls who are walking and texting will fall straight — bloop — into untreated sewage.

The workers who caused this debacle last week said they stepped away for two seconds to get orange cones to mark the site to warn pedestrians.

I'm betting the guys who pulled the girl out of the muck put on gas masks really fast, partly because of the smell but mostly because if that girl's dad saw how hard they were laughing, they'd be dead meat.

Especially because the teen's parents, according to Fox News, are now thinking of suing.

Well, of course.

It's not like we parents have time to teach our kids to look both ways before crossing the street *and* to actually look *at* it so they won't fall *through* it.

The government has to take some responsibility.

That's where the feds come in. If warning labels were required on cell phones, the monkey wouldn't be on the sewer guys' backs.

You know, something like: "Warning: Texting while walking may lead to isolation from social settings, ignorance of surroundings, distraction, absence of emotion, headaches, nausea, vomiting, psoriasis, plaque, restless leg syndrome, hardening of the arteries, complete respiratory failure, sudden death or falling into sewers."

Then, and only then, should the feds try something like padding signposts and sides of buildings and doorways, just in case one of our texting kids walks into them.

And maybe the government should consider changing "don't walk" signs from visual to audio, perhaps giving them the voice of an authoritative mom: "Yo, kid, I said put one more toe over that curb and you're going to be wearing a smaller shoe size."

That kind of thing.

We, as Americans, have to do whatever we can to keep our children safe.

Heaven forbid, they have to actually learn to watch where they are going.

'Tater Butt' available for corporate sponsorship

In Chattanooga, officials found a way to save public funds by having a private company fill the potholes in city streets. All they had to do was let the company paint "Refurbished by KFC" across the newly paved roads.

Not such a bad deal.

So I've got a proposal for KFC and I'll let them tattoo "Tummy tuck by KFC" right across my midsection in exchange.

I'll even wear a little diamond chicken leg belly-button ring.

For all you other corporate sponsors out there, I'm giving you notice my hindend is prime real estate that currently is large enough for a "Lipo by KFC" sign. After all, I hold the fried chicken franchise personally responsible for at least some of its spread. My dad didn't call me Tater Butt just because it sounded cute.

Well, it did kinda sound cute when it was hollered across the Walmart that time.

"Tater Butt, would you come to the Customer Service counter, please? Tater Butt?"

No need for a last name. What kid's going to answer to Tater Butt? Well, except me.

KFC did have a slight public relations problem with PETA, that group of animal rights activists — by which I mean people who have forgotten they are actually, well, people — who also wanted to pave potholes in Chattanooga and cover them with depictions of Col. Sanders as the devil. Poor ol' Col. Sanders. Give him a break. He died before he even knew it was wrong to stuff a bunch of chickens in cages on a big ol' truck.

Any-hoo, using private funds to better our public world could be a good thing.

Corporations already have taken over stadiums and arenas.

Think of the possibilities.

We could one day drive across McDonald's Bridge with its golden arches.

Our kids could be driven to school on Taco Bell buses.

And, let's be honest, ball fields could do with a better class of food. A little war between Chick-fil-A and Zaxby's could only benefit us parents, although, not, of course, our hindends.

If only La Z Boy would bid for the rights to the bleachers, we'd be all set.

And just think if Wal-Mart would sponsor schools. Teachers' eyes would glaze as they picture the endless supplies of glue, finger paints, and No. 2 pencils. And you could almost picture class moms' eyes tear up at the thought of all the paper towels and hand sanitizer … and maybe even a few pudding cups for when the days get a little stressful.

All I ask is that, if allowed to sponsor high schools, Burger King and McDonald's keep that freaky smiling king and weird red-headed clown off the football fields.

They scare the kids.

Not unlike my diamond chicken leg belly button ring would.

Me and the mayor are, like,
thisclose

Y'all know I'm not one to brag — much — but sometimes fame just lands on your doorstep and all you can do is say, "Boy, hydee, Fame. Come on in and bring your checkbook with you."

Last week, it was Hollywood. You all may be thinking it doesn't get much bigger than that.

But then the mayor invited me to be on his weekly radio show.

Yep. When I sat down in front of that hot mic in the showroom of the local Ford Lincoln Mercury dealership, I knew my life would never be the same.

This was almost as exciting as the time the reflection of my shirt ended up in a scene in a real-for-sure, made-it-to-the-silver-screen movie. My shirt acted alongside Zoe Saldana, who herself has acted alongside the likes of Johnny Depp and Ashton Kutcher. How's that for two degrees of separation?

But even then, when I watched my shirt flash before my eyes, I couldn't imagine I would one day be interviewed by MayorDan.

It's not everyone who can say she has been asked by her mayor to be friends on Facebook. I'll bet very few New Yorkers are asked to be friends with MayorMike. I'm just sayin.'

That's the great thing about a small town — we don't address our mayor as Mr. Williams or Mayor Williams or Mr. Mayor or even Hizzoner. He's MayorDan.

I'll bet even his wife calls him that.

Any-hoo, MayorDan had asked me to be on his Monday morning talk show on WKAC 1080 AM radio — broadcast from McClary Ford Lincoln Mercury with host Butch Menefee —mainly because I am such an interesting person with an exciting career … and no one else was willing to come on such short notice.

MayorDan asked about my early life, my college years, my career path — all scintillating stuff, as you can imagine — before he finally laid bare his true intent in asking me to be his guest: he wanted to delve further into the intimacies, er, intricacies of nakations, the subject of one of my recent columns.

That's right, MayorDan wanted to uncover the reasoning behind, as it were, the increasing popularity of nude resorts. Now I'm not saying there's anything inappropriate about MayorDan's interest, just that he was curious about why people go to resorts to get nekkid.

When I told him men were apparently required to wear bowties and cumberbunds at one resort's Nude Year's Eve event, he said, "I'm not sure where this is going…"

I could tell him: Nowhere good.

Changing the subject, he asked which of my columns had received the most response.

My answer was swift.

The one on mantyhose.

Hey, I don't make this stuff up.

When I explained mantyhose were pantyhose for men and most of the responses were from men who said they wore them and loved them — though there was that one guy with the fetish — the mayor pondered, his brow furrowed.

I'm not sure what he was picturing behind that brow but he did wonder aloud if any of his old pals who sit beside him at the lunch counter at Dub's Burgers — some of whose stomachs have benefited over the years from said burgers, if you catch my meaning — might have been wearing, unbeknownst to him, some mantyhose under their coverhalls.

Sometimes, I think inside MayorDan's head is not a place I want to visit.

I'm just sayin.'

Practically real people live in Beverly Hills

Y'all will never guess!

I have hobnobbed with the rich and famous. Well, not hobnobbed so much as gawked at the rich and famous.

Well, not gawked at the rich and famous so much as gawked at their locked gates and eight-foot tall hedges but there's no need to get technical.

What I'm trying to say is: People, I've been to Hollywood!

Yep, my daughter's high school dance team competed at a national competition in Anaheim, Calif., last weekend (won the whole thing, by the way) and, since my house was mortgaged to the rafters and my credit card was on life support and in need of prayers, me and some of the mamas said: Why not? Let's break out the big bucks and hit Rodeo Drive, by which we meant pay 50 bucks for a tour and walk around and take pictures of things we couldn't afford to buy.

Oh, and by the way, they do not hold bronco busting there. It is not *Roe-dee-oh* Drive. They call it Roe-*day*-oh Drive so you will know you won't find any horse manure there but you will find lots of snooty people who look like they've smelled horse manure whenever tourists walk past.

Even though they, in fact, work as sales clerks, they want you to know *they* work as sales clerks on Roe-*day*-oh Drive and therefore their lives are vastly more fulfilling than yours. After all, the clerk at Jimmy Choo may have touched Jennifer Aniston's heel and can you say that?

I walked into Louis Vuitton and marked myself as a tourist right away because I wasn't sure if my $30 jeans and Kohl's blouse would do the trick. I looked around at all the luggage and handbags — not one of which had a price tag — chose a small and, dare I say it, inexpensive looking keychain and asked, "How much?"

No one actually gasped but you could almost see the clerk choking one back. People apparently don't ask on Roe-*day*-oh Drive.

"Three-seventy-five," she said.

I wanted to ask, *"Cents?"* but one of the other moms hustled me on out of there before I could mark Alabama as totally fashion backward.

Any-hoo, our happy little van full of tourists also took a drive around Beverly Hills 90210. Did you know it's an actual city and not just a place they name a bunch of TV shows after?

Sure is. People actually live there.

At least I think they do. We didn't see people, just lots of perfection.

We saw Tom and Katie's driveway and hedges. They were nice. We saw the gate to the Playboy mansion and the roof of the house where Britney lived before she went off her nut. We got to see a few homes' exteriors in their entirety, like Dr. Phil's, Peter Falk's and Lucille Ball's (Lucy Arnaz lives there now, our driver said).

We also passed the house where the Osbournes reality show was filmed, when Ozzy, Sharon, Kelly and Jack showed the world their sick, er, special family bond. Our tour guide told us they bought another home for an upcoming show and Christina Aguilera lives in their old home. I wouldn't have wanted to see those carpet cleaning bills.

The day after we got back from California, I saw Sharon and Ozzy give an interview about their new show and the interviewer asked why they moved from Beverly Hills. Sharon said, basically, she was sick of all those tour buses driving past.

Well.

Maybe the Beverly Hills city council could start a Do Not Tour List, sort of like the Feds' Do Not Call List, and the buses could detour to some other home, like Weird Al Yankovic's or something.

Sharon probably really didn't like the tour buses because Ozzy kept wobbling out in front of them in his underwear muttering about going bat hunting and she had to keep chasing him down.

I'm just sayin.'

By the way, y'all, I'm starting a Louis Vuitton keychain fund. Send donations my way.

Chocolate emergency calls for action

Y'all know how Reader's Digest looks all cute and harmless?

Like a less strident little sibling to Time or Newsweek sitting on the newsstand for people who don't want big, stressful news with their Toaster Strudels and instant cappuccinos.

But I am here to tell you, just like little siblings, sometimes Reader's Digest can give you a bad news noogie that will turn your don't-worry-be-happy world upside down.

Here is the doomsday report I read in the July issue (please be sure there are no children in the room when you read this. Your reaction is likely to frighten them): "The cacao tree is battling a virus in the Ivory Coast, the world's largest producer, where crops could be down 33 percent, according to New Scientist."

Do you know what this means, people? Do you? That means the chocolate supply is about to drop 33 percent.

The *chocolate supply*.

When I was able to breathe again, I began to write this column. I knew I had to warn you, faithful readers. Well, right after I filled the pantry, two storage units, a garage and the attic with chocolate for my own self.

Don't tell me you wouldn't have done the same.

Let's be real here: Recessions come and recessions go. What is money really good for anyway? Paying bills, buying clothes, perhaps food for the children?

But can it buy happiness? Can it bring you Hugh Jackman?

No, more's the pity.

Chocolate, though, can make you forget, for a moment or two, that you'll never snuggle up next to Hugh on a mosquito-netted loveseat on a Tahitian island with soft music playing as he caresses your hair ... oh, OK, I'm back.

Chocolate is a remedy for nearly every stressful situation.

I should know. I am the official Chocolate in a Stressful Situation Tester — you can tell just by looking at me.

Chocolate has been known to remedy:

- A truly heinous date (even one when the guy brings his mother along, they slip on matching bowling shoes, then he asks *you* to pay).
- A horrific haircut like the one given to you by your 3-year-old the time she found your scissors when you were asleep.
- An especially stressful day at work (do the words "snack machine malfunction" mean anything to you?).
- The time the cat threw up on your new blouse and you didn't notice until you were already *at* the party.
- The time the dog died at the end of the movie. It's bound to happen in every dog movie, and a box of Goobers takes the edge off.
- The time you were at the pool with all the skinny moms and your float burst and you tried to make the best of it and blamed it on global warming and changing tides and alternating pressures and, sure, they all believed you.
- After you visited Graceland, saw the grave and were forced to admit Elvis really was dead.

So with the chocolate supply threatened, we need to stop wasting it on stupid stuff like kids birthday parties and those hollow chocolate Easter bunnies no one ever eats, except in extreme emergencies like when we run out of Goo Goo Clusters.

We've got to pour every last drop into our most important resource: distressed moms. Otherwise, think of the global explosion waiting to happen.

One day, just hours after the chocolate runs out, all the moms will begin drooling and grow catatonic.

That sure puts the "economic crisis" in perspective.

Who would change diapers, cook meals, do laundry?

So kids, go dig those old mini Snickers from beneath your beds and sofa cushions and scrape those classroom-reward Tootsie rolls from the bottoms of your backpacks. This is no time to be selfish.

Your moms need you.

Trust me. You'll understand someday when you're older.

Only the skilled can cover the 'critter beat'

Planning a career in journalism? Here's a tip: Skip the English classes in favor of biology, anatomy, zoology...oh, and maybe animal husbandry, too.

Journalism professors will tell you about the government beat, the crime beat and the education beat, but they keep one thing under wraps in hopes of retaining the few prospective journalists who weren't scared away when they heard the starting salary — the critter beat.

And be warned, potential Bob Woodwards, once you are assigned your first critter story, you unofficially become the "critter reporter" who covers the critter beat until death — or until you can figure out how to sucker the college intern into writing about the bat guano that is destroying a local landmark, thereby passing the torch.

Sometimes, though, a reporter may become an expert on a particular type of critter and then he or she won't easily shake the title.

In our newsroom, Karen is the Wild Hog Writer (Side note: "wild" modifies "hog," not "writer." Although sometimes...) Yep, after writing last year about a flurry of complaints from residents whose property was destroyed by a rowdy band of feral hogs, Karen is now assigned all wild pig stories.

You may think those would be few and far between but just last week, I had another call. I didn't even have to go into the newsroom and give a pop quiz to find out who was most knowledgeable — I had Karen right there wearing her Wild Hog Writer badge.

Then there was a call from a man about some roosters. This story was assigned to Jean, the All Things Fowl Writer. She earned the title when writing about chickens on the lam from the local poultry plant. In this case the roosters in question were, um, dead.

A reader said rooster carcasses being thrown beside the road near his home were scarred and had their feet filed to be fitted with spurs for illegal cockfighting, which, contrary to popular belief, we law-abiding Alabamians do not host on Grandma's front porch come a Saturday night.

Readers expect the same expertise when we write about critters as when covering NASA's space program over in Huntsville, so we try to educate ourselves on each critter we encounter. Sometimes, we fall short.

Which brings us to the Frozen Snake Incident.

When we received a call a few years back from local authorities saying a man housing venomous snakes had been arrested and his stash seized, a young writer took the sheriff at his word and reported the most venomous of the snakes, a type of cobra, had been euthanized using death-by-freezer (put into, not squashed beneath).

No one was thinking cobra popsicles could take the place of those pickle-juice pops sold at the ball field or anything; this was apparently just a tried-and-proven method of killing snakes among the badged population. (Guess none of the deputies had heard of the more common method of chopping them to death with a hoe.)

The onslaught of e-mails when the story hit nearly disabled my computer. Not only were the snake lovers of America (who knew there were so many?) incensed that the snake had been frozen but they pointed out that the particular type of cobra was not a danger to humans, never mind its 2-inch-long fangs and hypnotic death stare.

They were angry, not at authorities, but at us. As anyone knows, the entire newspaper staff — from the publisher to the tear-sheet clerk — is always in on any conspiracy, even the cover-up of the vile murder of an innocent cobra.

But some cover-ups benefit readers. Once, a reporter who had neglected to take a college course in reptile anatomy found herself needing to piece together the remains of a huge snake that had an unfortunate meeting with a haying machine. The thoughtful reader who had unwittingly dismembered the snake put each bloody piece in the back of a pickup and kindly drove it to our parking lot, rightly thinking this is the kind of thing that sells newspapers.

The reporter, looking at the scattered pieces, decided the resulting photo would be less likely to make readers lose their breakfasts if she assembled it into more of a completed-jigsaw snake than a snake in a blender, which, you have to admit, was prudent of her.

The good news is, one snake part looks pretty much like all the others.

The lesson, future journalists, is to be prepared to be dispatched to a scene of critter mayhem, such as the one where a woman and her child were recently trapped on the hood of their car, held hostage by a crazed raccoon we've nicknamed Cujo.

The resulting story? Soon to be a major motion picture.

Section 4

Lucy's got some splainin' to do
Or the joys of being owned by pets

Could cat whisperer help psycho-kitty?

Anyone know a cat whisperer?

I'm willing to give one of these special "animal communicators" a try if it will help me determine if our new cat Scout is seriously deranged or merely laughing behind his paw at our expense.

I need to know. It could affect whether he gets Fancy Feast or ValuTuna for the rest of his life.

Scout is a stray I found a few weeks ago roaming near Interstate 65. He's a beautiful boy — more tan than orange with strange, dark-gold eyes.

It's his adorable expression — cocked head, big innocent "love me" eyes — that made me take him home. It's that same expression, so far, that has saved him from sessions on the kitty therapist's tiny couch.

But he's walking a short piece of yarn.

Being a stray, Scout has the idea that he will never have enough food. I have the bite marks on my toes to prove he'll eat just about anything.

One day, I placed a half-empty can of Fancy Feast turkey dinner in a plastic, zippered bag. Knowing Scout's appetite, I placed the baggy high on a pantry shelf behind a box of cereal.

Within minutes, I heard the sound of bags of potato chips and boxes of Hamburger Helper falling to the floor. Running to the kitchen, I found Scout on the last shelf before the top, making his way toward the cat food.

He reminded me of myself when my daughter Shannon hides her Halloween candy from me.

I learned to firmly close the pantry door but there is no door to our kitchen. My sleep has so often been interrupted by crashing sounds that I no longer bother to get up to see what fell. I figure it will still be broken in the morning.

Nights are worse for Shannon, though. At some point in his 18-month lifetime, Scout must have experienced a terrible trauma at 4 a.m. Perhaps that was the time he was mugged by a crazed Chihuahua or a cat bully took his last stash of catnip.

Somehow, the combination of "4" and "a.m." turns him into a furry projectile with evil intent. That's when he slinks into Shannon's bedroom and oh-so-lovingly pounces on her feet and legs, scratching and clawing. If only he could wait an hour or so, he'd make a pretty good alarm clock. She might go to school covered in bandages but she'd get there on time.

I could live with these traits, I suppose, but I discovered a more, um, *disturbing* aspect of his personality. The other night, I was in Shannon's room when Scout hopped up on her bed and began kneading his favorite blanket. Then, as he kneaded, he grabbed a corner of the soft fabric between his teeth and began sucking it.

You read it right. I am the proud owner of a shelf-climbing, night stalking, blanky-sucking cat.

Of course, I am concerned only with Scout's mental health and not my public image. Oh, and Shannon says she is getting a little traumatized herself from sitting on her bed and finding it damp with cat spit.

So I need help. I went online and found a Web site for a cat whisperer who gave some advice for getting a cat to do what you want it to. For instance, by using your eyes, you can tell a cat where you want him to go.

This woman obviously doesn't know I have already told Scout where to go. Repeatedly.

But I decided to give her advice a try. I read: "When you want your cat to come to you, or jump up on your lap, make eye contact for about two seconds, then shift your eyes to look where you want the cat to end up. Then immediately shift your eyes back to make eye contact with your cat, hold for one second, then look somewhere else. You may have to do this two or three times before your cat understands that you understand the whole 'eye thing.'"

Sounded good.

Eye contact. Cheap. Simple. Won't keep me from my Andy Griffith reruns on TV.

I called Scout several times but he apparently has not learned his name (which I'm sure the cat whisperer would attribute to the fact that I call him Butthead with such frequency. Hey, it just slips out.).

So I sat cross-legged on the floor and sat Scout a few inches in front of me. I stared — one-thousand-one, one-thousand-two —then looked away.

When I looked back, Scout was tangled in the cord of a lamp, which teetered precariously on the side table. I grabbed it just in time.

After untangling him, I tried again. I looked at Scout then oh-so-casually looked where I wanted him to end up, my lap.

This time, he took the hint, but he may have misinterpreted the subtlety of my signal. I'll let you know when I get the bandages removed from my thigh.

Giving up, I headed to bed, ignoring the sound of Scout eating the plastic decorations that adorn my daughter's shower curtain.

Somewhere out there, I know there is help.

Or maybe I should fall back on the time-tested technique for owners of Pets with Issues — ear plugs and a blindfold.

Blanky-sucking cat is stealing hearts

Well, we survived our first year with Scout, the shelf-climbing, night-stalking, blanky-sucking cat my daughter and I adopted last October.

The official score is: Scout, 16. Us, 0.

Here is a detailed tally:

Broken glasses, 6.

Broken plates, 2.

Broken perfume bottles, 1.

Ruined window blinds, 2.

De-sequined shower curtain, 1.

Items lost in an area known as the Scout Triangle behind the corner entertainment center, undetermined (but at least 5).

I have to admit, not all the carnage can be blamed on Scout, the tan stray with big, gold love-me eyes we found roaming near Interstate 65.

If we'd learned after the first one — or even two — broken drinking glasses that anything left on our kitchen counter constituted prey, we would still have enough for company. As it is, we are forced to take out the plastic Beauty and the Beast cup when we have more than two people over.

These days, I don't hear as much crashing in the middle of the night, but if my teenage daughter Shannon leaves open the door to her bathroom, we soon will hear the sounds of clinking bottles as Scout moves across her shelves to find a spot high on her shower curtain where he hasn't eaten the large sequin decorations, sort of like a giraffe foraging ever higher to find areas of the trees that still have leaves.

And Scout doesn't understand why we girls feel the need to close the window blinds at night. He climbs through the slats, which, in at least two instances, has left holes that can be seen from the road.

While he is now secure enough to sleep on our beds rather than on top of the refrigerator, he continues to feel the need to look down on us from high places.

Last weekend, Shannon and I were about to put her great-grandmother's porcelain nativity scene in its special place atop the entertainment center before we came to our senses.

"How could we live with ourselves if Baby Jesus ended up in the Scout Triangle, never to be seen again?" she said.

I was more worried Baby Jesus would be end up in Scout's Tummy, which would be difficult to explain not only to Great Grandmother and the veterinarian, but to the pastor.

Scout also seems to have passed the stage where he feels the need to suck a corner of Shannon's favorite soft blanket, leaving her to find surprise wet spots when she got into bed.

Unfortunately, he substituted another oral fixation — paper chewing.

To Scout, the hum of the printer is more seductive than catnip. If we don't grab the paper the minute it comes out, he will devour it. Shannon is now among the few students known to have said to her teacher: "The cat ate my homework."

Last time Shannon had a slumber party, the girls ate the large pizza with cheese and Scout ate the large box — with relish.

And though he still hasn't adjusted to the time change and wakes me for breakfast at 4:30 every morning, I must admit, I'd forgive Scout most anything.

The tally, I guess, wasn't quite right.

I forgot to add: Hearts stolen, 2.

How to be owned by a cat

Cats are nature's most perfect creatures. I should know — my cat told me.

Of course I talk to my cat. Don't you?

What's that? Your cat doesn't talk back?

Oh, but she does. You probably just need a few pointers on how to listen.

I have spent a lot of time communicating with Luvey and she says I am a better human because of it.

The first requirement is that you must love your cat unconditionally. An example: You've been awakened by a brush of whiskers against your cheek and you inadvertently scream, causing your cat to jump three feet and land on your face, yet you merely wipe the blood from your eyes and go get the Fancy Feast. The stitches can wait until Fluffy has eaten.

The next requirement is that you can read signals. You see your cat "making biscuits" — what we Southern cat lovers call it when cats knead the sofa cushions with their front paws — and immediately sense your cat is open to a good neck massage. Or your cat awakens from a 12-hour nap near the fireplace, stretches, yawns and fixes you with a cold stare and you sense he is ready for dinner.

For instance, the other day I said while rubbing Luvey, "Hey, you crazy ol' girl. You've gained a few, haven't you?"

Right away, I knew I had broken at least three important by-laws of cat ownership: 1) Questioned her mental health, 2) drew attention to the fact that she is (how to put it?) not as svelte as she once was and 3) interrupted her during a yawn. I immediately made amends by going out and catching some fresh tuna for her dinner.

If you are in tune with your cat's signals, you are ready to listen. Use the following guide to help until you get the hang of it:

• A sharp "Nyah" (uttered upon being awakened by your selfish desire to sneeze):

Translation: "Who are you and why are you breathing my air?"

• A disgruntled "Nyah" (after having her dinner-plate-sized butt slid from atop your open book)

Translation: "Oh, were you reading that?"

• A steady purr (while being rubbed in that special spot just under his chin)

Translation: "Humans do have their uses."

• MRRR-OWW! MRRR-OWW!

Translation: "Just wanted to let you know it's 2 a.m. Do you know where your Meow Mix is?"

• An insistent "meo-o-o-w, meo-o-ow" (while blocking your entry into the house)

Translation: "You couldn't have called? You know dinner is at 5 sharp."

• An unwavering gaze followed by a slow blink.

Translation: "You didn't really think I was going to eat that supermarket-brand, meat by-product, did you?"

Life is much smoother — and less dangerous — for humans who learn to communicate with their cats. Luvey and I have lived together for 11 years and I am proud to say I have never stood in the way of her independence — or her food dish.

The Unfortunate Christmas Cockatoo Confrontation

In the nightmare, I was running in slow motion down the hallway of my aunt's house, hair flowing behind me, heart racing as my attacker closed in. Within seconds, I would be flat on the ground, facing certain bodily harm from the foot-high cockatoo waddling behind me, feathers flared frighteningly around her beak, which was opened slightly, ready to cut me to ribbons...

OK, it wasn't a dream. The events described above occurred when my daughter and I went to Georgia for a family Christmas gathering, and are now known as the Unfortunate Christmas Cockatoo Confrontation.

Just to end the suspense...I survived to write this column. But barely.

It all started when we arrived at Aunt Beverly's in Macon and she had set up the palatial cage in the guest room for Barney, who was named before her sex was determined, which goes a long way toward explaining her anger management problem.

Shannon's first thought was to take out Barney and play with her, by which I mean allowing her to use her huge, strong claws to walk from your shoulder, across your head and down your chest where she nestles and nudges, wanting to have her plumage rubbed. We'd done this many times in the past with no bloodshed at all.

But we didn't know two things this day:

• Barney had recently injured her beak by falling from a high place and was now afraid of high places (I *know* she's a bird, for pity's sake.)

• To Barney, a towel acts as a red cape does to a bull.

Had we known, we may not have been as nonchalant when Aunt Beverly decided to go to the grocery store, leaving us *alone with the bird*.

For a few minutes, Shannon held Barney on her arm and petted her feathers while Barney made happy bird noises. At least I think that's what they were.

The mood changed when we decided we needed to freshen up and went to put Barney in her cage.

I reached to take Barney from Shannon, who with her bird senses had divined our evil plot, and she dug her beak into my forearm.

For those who have never had a cockatoo beak dug into their forearms, it's like being bitten by a pair of hedge clippers. In pain, I flung my arm, which upset Barney, who retaliated by slicing open my finger with her beak.

"Yoo-o-o-w!" I screamed. Somehow, Barney was on the floor. When my panicked eyes found Barney's, I froze.

At this point, a part of my brain decided I would no longer make fun of actress Karen Black for her role in the 1970s horror movie "Trilogy of Terror," in which she spends 30 minutes running from an 18-inch high wooden warrior statue that came to life and terrorized her with a kitchen knife. Never again would I so callously think, "What's the worst he could do—slice up her ankles?"

The thought of Barney's beak on my delicate ankles sent me running. She waddled after me, menacingly.

Finally, I hopped on the bed, pulling two pillows in front of me as a barricade.

I couldn't see Barney on the floor. I held my breath.

Suddenly, she jumped up on the bed and raced as fast as her pigeon-toed claws would take her toward my barricade.

"Shannon, help!"

I screamed.

I really did.

Shannon tried catching Barney with a towel, to which Barney responded by bloodying my knuckles.

What happened next is a blur, but Barney was safely in her cage by the time Aunt Beverly came home.

Later, after we told her about Barney's attack, we could hear Beverly in the guest room, speaking in her "plantation Southern" accent in a tone reserved for babies and puppies: "Has Barney been a bad bird? Were you a bad girl, Barney? You know we don't bite our people."

After a couple of bandages and an eggnog — or was that a bandage and a couple of eggnogs? — I was fine.

After all, what's a family Christmas without a few scars?

Dog shows wasted on the dogs

Dog shows are wasted on the dogs.

I mean, they live to obediently trot beside their masters, look cute in exchange for treats and have their butts rubbed by guys in tuxedos.

Where's the challenge?

With dogs, you get women in boring suits and rubber-soled shoes jogging jauntily around a ring.

You get announcers with unnaturally deep voices intoning how ancient and reliable and family friendly the breed is.

You get judges with furrowed brows struggling to determine which incredibly adorable canine is the most incredibly adorable.

You get a white toy poodle so coiffed she looks like she's trying to escape from a bubble bath gone horribly awry.

Yawn.

Why not try this show with, say, cats?

Now there's some entertainment waiting to happen.

Firstly, cats do love to preen. Which other animal spends 16 hours of each day sleeping and the other eight licking itself clean? Getting beauty sleep and grooming are a cat's only responsibilities.

Showing off before judges comes naturally, but these are not please-love-me types. Cats will not be cute on command.

Think of the entertainment value when a fancy feline — tiring of the crowd, the noise, the tux guy feeling her butt— reaches out a dainty paw to slice his index finger.

Then, her work done, she sits and licks said weapon of mass destruction, er, paw, refusing to budge from the judging perch because, after all, perches are much like thrones.

Once a call is made to paramedics (who have never been needed, of course, at a ho-hum dog show) and they have finished bandaging the judge, the cat will watch as three men in jumpsuits approach her, ready to forcibly remove her. When they are within a whisker of her, ready to lunge, she will calmly leap to the ground and complete her walk before the audience. The men, along with the judge, will be left in a puddle on the ground.

And cats are not about to let some other prissy feline upstage them — there are sure to be some hissing contests.

And as the producers of Dynasty know, catfights sell.

Way more fun than dogs.

But dog shows do have their moments. I have to admit I became engrossed last week in watching the Westminster Kennel Club show on TV.

I saw breeds from Kuvasz to Shiba Inus to Pekingese to Bleu Cheese. I saw dogs 10 inches tall to nearly four feet tall, which I have to admit would be a record height for a cat. I have never seen the cat yet that could stand on the floor and put his paws on my shoulders, though I do have a few scars there from the time Scout jumped me from the bookshelf.

It's amazing what you can learn — besides the fact that people look funny running in suits and sensible shoes.

Did you know some dogs are part duck? Didn't think so. Otterhounds, it turns out, have webbed feet so they can hunt, surprise, otter.

And did you realize you could measure your 3-year-old child against the ear-span of a coonhound, whose long floppy ears can be about 35 inches from tip to tip. I'd hate to see the Q-Tip that would clean those babies.

Just don't ask me which breed won.

I also learned those deep announcer voices have an oddly soothing effect that can lull you into a restful night's sleep.

Unless you are one of those people lucky enough to be owned by cats — then you can sleep only until they say so.

Cats and teens: Who knew they had so much in common?

Summer has flown by — at least for kids. To them, it came and went before they could text message: "That was it?"

Moms, though, will revel in the peace the first day of school brings.

No more calls while you're at work to ask, "Is the cat's vomit supposed to be green?" or "Joey's turning blue. Is that a bad thing?"

No more rushing home from a long day so you can drive them to sleepovers, camps or games.

No more waking up at midnight to the sound of her bedroom TV blaring loud enough to wake Mom, the neighbors and astronauts in the sky lab — but not the teenager or the cat sleeping peacefully 6 feet away.

It occurred to me teens are like cats in other ways.

Both sleep 16 hours a day, typically not the same hours you are trying to sleep, which leads me to my next point:

Both are nocturnal. A teen will stay up until 2 a.m. just in case that cute boy decides to send a photo of himself to her cell phone. A cat will stay up until 2 a.m. just so he can be at the foot of the bed, claws at the ready, when you move your foot beneath the covers.

Both have selective hearing. A teen can hear her cell phone vibrating with a text message from two rooms away but won't hear the buzz of an alarm clock resting on the bed beside her head. A cat can sleep through the sounds of three teens pillow fighting above him but will hear the pop of a can of cat food from a distance of two miles.

Both are hunters — when they want to be. A teen will spend days hunting a pair of strategically torn jeans and perfectly shrunken and faded T-shirt to make a good impression on the first day of school but can't find her tennis shoes for PE class when they're on her feet. A cat can occupy hours skillfully stalking a reflection on the living room wall but will overlook the centipede that made its way into your closet and the toe of your shoe.

Both are stubborn. Ask a teen to get off the sofa and empty the dishwasher and she will say, "Okay," and not move. For three days. Tell a cat to get off the sofa and he'll give a look that says, "You and what animal control officer are gonna make me?" and not move. For three days.

I would add more to the list but the cat is batting at my pen and the teen needs help finding her purse.

I might tell her it's hanging on her shoulder — right after I take a nap.

Where are tear-jerker films about cats?

"Marley and Me," like most movies about lovable dogs that won't follow the rules, is a big smash at the box office.

I can understand why. When I read the book, I bawled like a baby over the last 20 pages.

You never see movies about cats, but, take my word for this, they can make you cry — and not in a good way.

Cats, like Marley, avoid rules, but not because they have learning disabilities or even attention deficit disorder.

Felines seem to have the same attitude as Richard Nixon who was famously quoted as saying "When the President does it, it's not illegal."

When a cat does it, it's not against the rules.

Simple as that.

At our house, Scout is the most Marley-like, by which I mean psychotic.

Our two other cats, the twins Luvey and Mad Max, have never jumped on a counter, scratched the furniture or peed on anything that shouldn't be peed upon.

They come when they are called.

They sleep on my bed in a heart shape, heads together, sleek, black bodies curved and tails coming together in a point.

They are perfect cats.

As for Scout … it's a good thing he's so cute.

He thinks he rules our house, which is why I like to call him Butthead, er, Scout Master.

He rules mainly because, well, he's the biggest and the one most in need of Ritalin, which is typical of what makes a successful ruler.

He's known to wake humans or feline siblings from a deep slumber by leaping across the room and using their bodies as a springboard, leaving behind scratch marks and blood drops and making the sleeping body go "A-a-ackkkk!," which also is typical of what makes a successful ruler.

He climbs shelves, knocking heirlooms to the floor and leaving a dusting of buff-colored fur on every surface.

Thursday night, when my daughter Shannon and I were watching a scary movie on TV, we heard a strange scratching from her bathroom.

I checked, but found nothing.

After sitting back down, right at a jump-out-of-your-seat moment, we heard the noise again.

Again, I saw nothing in the bathroom. I was about to determine we had a ghost, when Shannon decided to open the 10-inch wide drawer in the bathroom vanity, where the noise seemed to originate.

There, among Q-tips, bottles of nail polish and cotton balls, sat our muscular, 15-pound Scout. He didn't even have the sense to look guilty. He popped up as if to say, "Anyone for a manicure? No? Alrighty then."

He somehow turned and exited the back of the drawer using the same manner he apparently used to get in — by crawling out the bottom of the vanity, through a space that looked to be about the size of a Matchbox car.

Scout comes running when I pull warm sheets from the dryer — his Kitty Sense tells him when the laundry contains sheets and not unmentionables or socks — and leaps to the center of the bed, waiting to be "made up" into it.

Sometimes he'll stay tucked beneath the sheets for hours, likely contemplating world peace, his stash of catnip or the hairball he just coughed up. I'll forget he's there, then notice the lump in my bed and rush to be sure he hasn't suffocated under the pile of sheets and blankets.

For royalty, he doesn't always come across as dignified — or smart. But then, neither does Prince Charles.

By the way, Luvey and Max don't know they aren't in charge. Don't tell them, kay?

We finally live in some semblance of peace and harmony because — since Shannon became a teen — everybody thinks he or she rules the house.

Except me. I am under no such delusions. If I ruled the house, I would be sunning on a windowsill watching birds in the yard and having my stomach rubbed instead of washing dishes and folding laundry.

Or maybe I'd just stay tucked beneath warm sheets, contemplating my next meal.

Cats vs. dogs: Dogs have some splainin' to do

I have been accused in the past of not being a dog person.

This is not true.

My first pet was a beagle and he was the best dog *ever*. Well, he must have had some wiener dog in him because his legs were about two inches long and his stomach and ears dragged the ground but still, he was the best dog *ever* that couldn't run very fast and whose stomach and ears dragged the ground.

But as an adult, I am basically the whichever-pet-requires-the-least-amount-of-exertion-on-my-part person. Which is why I have cats.

My existence was quite ordered until my teen daughter Shannon brought home a stray beagle-mix pup the other day and, of course, it was going to be put to *death* if we did not keep it.

We, the Kazek family, were the only ones on the planet who stood between this poor defenseless puppy and certain annihilation.

And, to my relief, Shannon was more than willing to take on ALL the responsibilities herself — feeding, bathing, walking, training … acclimating the puppy to the three cats. Whew. *That* made me feel better.

My cats have the dog-like qualities I need — they come when I call, sleep on my bed, pout when I've been out of town — without all that dumb, slobbery dog stuff.

When is the last time you saw a cat sitting at your feet, leash in her mouth, wagging her entire body excitedly, emitting a tiny stream of piddle, until, after eight or nine hours, you feel guilty enough to get up and take her for a walk?

And when did you ever have to take a cat out in the back yard when it's 14 degrees, uttering stupid phrases like "Come on, baby, do your business," or "Go poo-poo for Mommy," "Please, please go potty," — at this point tears have frozen to your face — and then finally "You better go or I'm gonna *#!@#" and then the neighbors call the police and it turns into a whole incident that never would have happened if you had an animal that went poo in a litter box.

Cats do not have to sniff the entire square footage of a yard before deciding exactly which spot has the perfect aroma to leave their pee.

They do not have to make a dizzying 18 gazillion circles before they can squat.

Cats do not bite their own tails.

Cats do not learn to stay or sit, for the same reason I don't — they don't want to.

However, we have a cat named Butthead, er, Scout, I will admit has a few psychological problems — he loves to eat paper. Shannon was only kid in school who ever had to tell her teacher, "The cat ate my homework." I was supposed to send a note saying she was telling the truth but Scout ate it.

The puppy — which Shannon appropriately named Lucy, as in "Looo-cy, you got some splainin' to do" — loves wood. She's already chewed a paint stirrer she found in the garage, the coffee table and an antique rocker, and whenever we are outdoors her favorite items are landscaping ties, sticks and tree bark. Not that I'm saying she's dumb.

And while cats may have the same tendency as dogs to scratch and chew things they are not supposed to, they have the good sense to not look guilty about it so that sometimes we cat owners might actually wonder if we did it ourselves.

"Scout, are you the one who ate the newspaper?"

And Scout would sit imperially, lift his chin and look at me as if to say, "Do I *look* stupid enough to eat paper?" until I would begin to think, "Mmmm. Maybe *I* ate it. I was awfully hungry when I got home from work."

But a dog looks guilty before you even realize it's done anything.

Lucy will come flouncing over to the foot of my chair and look up with big amber eyes and I'll say, "What have you done?" and go looking for a mess.

On Thursday, I found a trail made of pieces of a chewed ink pen and began to panic.

Sure enough, the trail ended in a big black stain right in the middle of the living room carpet. I guess I could hang a photo there and tell guests I'm trying feng shui.

I've never seen a cat eat an ink pen. Even Scout.

A puppy's a good argument for teen abstinence

All the years I'd kept Shannon from having a puppy just because I knew it would pee on my carpet, claw my furniture and chew my shoes, I never knew it would be so invaluable for teaching that most important high school lesson — abstinence.

Trust me, and I'm sure any parent of a teen would agree, the consequences-of-sex lesson is worth every pair of shoes and one-of-a-kind family heirloom our new puppy has digested over the last three weeks.

Despite early heartfelt promises — "I'll feed her. I'll walk her every day. Pleasepleasepleasepleasepleasepleasepleasepleaseplease let me keep her." — after just two weeks with her beagle puppy Lucy, Shannon had grown weary of the responsibilities of being a "parent."

She no longer liked being awakened at 5 a.m., especially in summer when sleepovers might keep her up until 2. She no longer liked scrubbing yellow stains from the carpet or having her feet continually damp from being licked.

Still, she diligently walked and fed and played and made a good puppy mama. But before long, our house began to sound like the toy aisle in Walmart: "No, Lucy." "Put that down!" "How did you manage to fit that in your mouth?" "If you do that again, I'll …" "Get that Tinkertoy out of your nose."

Well, that last one, maybe not so much.

Shannon began to appear tired.

Her clothes looked worn and slept in.

Oh, they were.

Any-hoo. She began to smell of kibble and pat her boyfriend on the head.

The strain was showing.

But she wasn't ready to admit parenting Lucy was too much for her.

Not even when Lucy:

• chewed one heel of each of three pairs of my good shoes;

• shredded the underside of the upholstered chair in the living room;

• ate the tassels from a decorative cushion;

• buried a (damp) rawhide bone in the kitty litter, then dug it up and reburied in my lingerie drawer;

• gnawed my $50 bra;

• chewed my purse strap;

• uprooted two plants;

• ingested three books;

• broke an ink pen on the carpet;

• chewed the legs of an antique rocking chair that belonged to my parents.

No, Shannon remained steadfast through the loss of all my personal property.

Then one day she called me at work.

"I'm gonna kill this dog!" she hollered.

"Calm down," I told her. "What'd she do that was so terrible?"

"She *ate* my cell phone."

Though I would prefer life lessons such as these to occur on my $20 phone rather than her $200 phone, I suppose then they would not be life lessons.

Lucy had now taken away Shannon's ability to communicate with her friends, flirt with boys, order pizza and update her Facebook page — in short, to breathe.

"OK, then," I said calmly. "Let's get rid of the dog."

"No-o-o-o," Shannon wailed.

"Then you'd better call and complain to someone who didn't just spend $500 making the backyard into K9-0210 and who isn't wearing shoes with one heel shorter than the other and whose underwire isn't biting into her ribcage right now."

So she called to complain to her friends — I assume she had to relearn how to use a landline — and, when I got home from work, I carefully explained to Shannon how babies are 18 gabillion times more trouble than puppies.

"Really?" she asked.

"Well, yeah. You can't even let them pee in the yard. My friend Alissa? Her son peed in the kitchen sink once."

"Uck."

"Even worse … at some point, no matter how hard you try, kids learn to talk. Remember that time when you were 3 and you asked, really loud, why that lady's thighs had dents in them? You wondered if she'd been in a wreck or something?"

She seemed to mull this over. "So how long before you have to stop training kids?"

"Oh, 'bout 25, 30 years. Depends," I tell her.

"That long, huh?"

"That long."

"Guess I'll stick with the dog."

And my work here is done.

About the Author

Photo by Kim Rynders

Kelly Kazek is managing editor of The News Courier in Athens, Alabama, where she has encountered a cow with a strategically placed fifth leg, a man claiming to be Elvis' illegitimate son and witnesses to UFOs. Her humor column has been syndicated to newspapers across the country. She has won more than 100 state and national press awards. She lives in northern Alabama with her daughter, who is continually embarrassed by her mother's columns and who is plotting revenge.